COLLEGIALITY AND SERVICE FOR TENURE AND BEYOND

Acquiring a Reputation as a Team Player

Franklin Silverman

Westport, Connecticut
London

Library of Congress Cataloging-in-Publication Data

Silverman, Franklin H., 1933–
    Collegiality and service for tenure and beyond : acquiring a reputation as a team player /
Franklin Silverman.
        p.   cm.
    Includes bibliographical references (p.) and index.
    ISBN 0–89789–913–X (alk. paper)
    1. College teachers—Tenure—Handbooks, manuals, etc.   2. College teachers—Promotions—
Handbooks, manuals, etc.   3. College teachers—Professional relationships—Handbooks, manuals,
etc.   I. Title.
  LB2335.7.S548   2004
  378.1′21—dc22   2003057990

British Library Cataloguing in Publication Data is available.

Library of Congress Catalog Card Number: 2003057990
ISBN: 0–89789–913–X

First published in 2004

Praeger Publishers, 88 Post Road West, Westport, CT 06881
An imprint of Greenwood Publishing Group, Inc.
www.praeger.com

Printed in the United States of America

The paper used in this book complies with the
Permanent Paper Standard issued by the National
Information Standards Organization (Z39.48–1984).

10   9   8   7   6   5   4   3   2   1

CONTENTS

PREFACE

This book is the third in a series of candid handbooks intended to provide assistant professors and graduate students contemplating a career in academia much of the practical information they'll need to maximize the likelihood of being tenured and promoted to associate professor. The first book in this series (Silverman, 1999) dealt with the publication and scholarship component of the requirements for achieving these goals, and the second (Silverman, 2001) dealt with the teaching component. This book deals with the two remaining components—collegiality and service. It is, to the best of my knowledge, the first book to have these as its primary focus.

While this book is likely to be most helpful to nontenured faculty and graduate students who are contemplating a career in academia, much of the information presented in it can also help tenured faculty and full- or part-time instructors who don't have a tenure-track appointment to survive and prosper. With regard to the latter, the information provided herein can facilitate their ability to function in ways that will convince their department to continue offering them annual contracts.

It's difficult to win a game without having a working knowledge of its rules and strategies. Getting promoted from assistant professor to associate professor and being tenured can be viewed as a game that has both rules and strategies.

By viewing survival in academia as a game, I'm not intending to demean it. I've been a college teacher for more than 35 years. I'm viewing it in this way because I've found when mentoring junior faculty that doing so makes the dynamics of the process more understandable to them.

Also, to play a game successfully, you must understand its unwritten rules and strategies as well as its written ones. Unfortunately, there is a risk of appearing cynical when you describe a game's unwritten rules. But my goal is for this book to be as helpful as I can make it, and so I tried to deal with the subject as honestly and as completely as I could.

It isn't possible to give credit to the many sources from which the ideas in this book have been drawn. This book is the result of more than 35 years of involvement with college teaching and the tenure process as well as hundreds of hours of conversations with persons in academia about issues pertaining to them, particularly faculty at Marquette University and members of the Text and Academic Authors Association. Thus, I cannot credit this or that idea to a specific person, but I can say "thank-you" to all whose ideas I have borrowed.

Franklin H. Silverman, Ph.D.

Chapter 1

BE COLLEGIAL OR PERISH!

Your success in academia will be determined, in large part, by how well you meet your department and institution's expectations for teaching, scholarship (i.e., research and publishing), and service (i.e., largely evincing collegiality). I dealt with meeting those expectations for teaching and scholarship in three previous books (Silverman, 1998, 1999, 2001). I'll be focusing in this book on meeting those for service.

Academia, unfortunately, isn't an ivory tower. That is, being respected as a scholar and a teacher isn't all that's usually required for being promoted and tenured. Unless a scholar has secured large amounts of extramural funding for his or her institution and is likely to continue doing so, it's almost always necessary for him or her to also be perceived as being a team player (evincing collegiality). While a reputation as a team player is unlikely to compensate for a weak teaching or publication record in promotion and tenure decisions, not having one can nullify an adequate, but marginal, publication and teaching record for such decisions. In fact, a lack of collegiality that's regarded as being substantial can nullify even a relatively strong teaching and publication record. Few departments would have much enthusiasm for granting tenure to an assistant professor who refused to do his or her fair share of essential service tasks (e.g., student advising and recruitment) even if that person had an exceptionally strong teaching and publication record. The reason, of course, is that other faculty in the department would have to do more of them.

The negative impact of a perceived lack of collegiality on a career in academia isn't limited to junior faculty. Two other groups whose careers in academia can be adversely affected by a perceived lack of collegiality are associate professors and part- and full-time instructors.

A perceived lack of collegiality can affect the career of an associate professor in a number of ways. It can, for example, affect his or her bid for promotion to full professor, particularly if the candidate's post-tenure publication, teaching, and/or extramural funding records are marginal. A colleague of mine recently was denied support for promotion to full professor at the college level primarily for this reason. It wasn't, however, mentioned in the committee report because of fear of litigation. My university, unlike some, does not specifically mention a lack of collegiality in its faculty handbook as a reason for denying promotion or tenure. The reasons given in the report were a marginal post-tenure teaching, publication, and extramural funding record.

Two other ways that a perceived lack of collegiality can adversely affect the career of an associate professor are he or she receiving relatively small merit salary increases and/or relatively large (or otherwise undesirable) teaching loads. At some institutions (including mine) all salary increases are based on merit. One way that an institution can "encourage" tenured faculty to resign or retire is by giving them salary increases that they're unlikely to consider respectable. Another is giving them a teaching load that they're likely to dislike because of its size and/or subject matter.

The need for collegiality for survival in academia isn't limited to tenure-track faculty. It also pertains to part- and full-time instructors. Not surprisingly, an instructor whom a department regards as lacking in collegiality is less likely than otherwise to continue receiving contracts.

WHAT IS COLLEGIALITY IN ACADEMIA?

Collegiality in academia can be defined in a number of ways. Perhaps the most meaningful is how it's perceived by a department's faculty. What might you do that at least some in your department are likely to interpret as evincing or not evincing collegiality? Table 1 contains a partial list of such behaviors, some of which are directly and others indirectly linked to collegiality. Almost all, incidentally, are dealt with elsewhere in the book.

The behaviors mentioned in Table 1 are directly or indirectly linked to service to one's department, college, university, community, or profession. You evince collegiality, in part, by accepting responsibility for

Table 1
Behaviors that at least some in your department are likely to interpret as evincing or not evincing collegiality

Evincing Collegiality	Not Evincing Collegiality
Attending almost all departmental and college faculty meetings	Frequently missing departmental and college faculty meetings
Being willing to direct theses and other student research	Whenever possible, refusing to direct theses and other student research that isn't directly related to your own
Willingly writing students letters of recommendation for graduate school or jobs	Discouraging students from asking you for letters of recommendation for graduate school or jobs
Being willing to do your fair share of student advising	Attempting to wiggle out of doing your fair share of student advising
Directing as much (or more) of your time and energy to your average students as you do to your better students	Investing as little as possible of your time and energy in your average students
Doing your fair share of departmental committee work	Investing as little as possible of your time and energy in departmental committee work
Being respectful of the faculty in your department, particularly the senior faculty	Being disrespectful toward the faculty in your department, particularly the senior faculty
With regard to awards and publications, maintaining a low profile in your department and a high profile with your dean and other upper administrators	With regard to awards and publications, maintaining a high profile in your department and a low profile with your dean and other upper administrators
Not being a chronic complainer, particularly to your chairperson	Being a chronic complainer, particularly to your chairperson
Becoming enmeshed in departmental politics only when it's necessary to do so defensively	Becoming enmeshed in departmental politics
Demanding only your fair share of departmental resources	Demanding more than your fair share of departmental resources
Willingly participating in your fair share of student recruitment activities	Refusing to participate in your fair share of student recruitment activities
Spending very little of the time that you're on campus "gossiping" with colleagues	Spending a significant percentage of the time that you're on campus "gossiping" with colleagues

Table 1
Behaviors that at least some in your department are likely to interpret as evincing or not evincing collegiality (continued)

Evincing Collegiality	Not Evincing Collegiality
Using "I'd appreciate it if..." rather than "I want..." language when making requests of colleagues	Using "I want..." rather than "I'd appreciate it if..." language when making requests of colleagues
Becoming actively involved in your state or national professional association(s) and volunteering to serve on committees, and doing your fair share of work while on them	Avoiding involvement with your state or national professional association(s), including their committees
Becoming actively involved as a volunteer in your community—for example, giving occasional free lectures to local service organizations	Avoiding community involvement when you do not benefit personally from it (e.g., receive an honorarium)
Volunteering to serve on college and institutional committees and while on them doing your fair share of the work	Avoiding serving on college and institutional committees
Being available and helpful to students outside of the classroom	Minimizing academic involvement with students outside of the classroom
Seeking research and other types of collaboration with colleagues in your "territory" when doing so can be beneficial	Resisting research and other types of collaboration with colleagues in your "territory" even when doing so can be beneficial
Being helpful to colleagues when they make reasonable requests	Avoiding being helpful to colleagues when they make reasonable requests unless you'll benefit from doing so
Not being a "pain in the ass" to have around	Being a "pain in the ass" to have around
Establishing a reputation for being dependable (e.g., usually meeting deadlines)	Failing to establish a reputation for being dependable (e.g., rarely meeting deadlines)
Conducting yourself on the job in a professional manner when it is important to do so	Often failing to conduct yourself on the job in a professional manner when it is important to do so
Conducting yourself in a manner that makes it unlikely you'll be accused of sexual harassment	Often failing to conduct yourself in a manner that makes it unlikely you'll be accused of sexual harassment

Table 1
Behaviors that at least some in your department are likely to interpret as evincing or not evincing collegiality (continued)

Evincing Collegiality	Not Evincing Collegiality
Conducting yourself in a manner that makes it unlikely you'll be accused of cultural insensitivity	Often failing to conduct yourself in a manner that makes it unlikely you'll be accused of cultural insensitivity
Being yourself—not a stereotype of how you believe a professor should behave	Projecting a professorial "image" that isn't compatible with your personality
Applying for extramural funding that can be helpful to both you and your department (e.g., that could support a graduate assistantship)	Applying for extramural funding that's almost entirely self-serving
Behaving in ways that are likely to significantly enhance the reputation of your department, college, university, and profession, as well as your own	Behaving in ways that are likely to significantly enhance your reputation, but only minimally those of your department, college, university, and profession
Being proactive in making yourself available to the media when there is an opportunity to enhance the reputation of your department, college, university, or profession	Not being proactive with the media when there is an opportunity to enhance the reputation of your department, college, university, or profession
Not demanding (but being grateful for) a reduction in your faculty (e.g., teaching) load if you're expected to publish	Demanding a reduction in your faculty (e.g., teaching) load if you're expected to publish
Usually being willing to come to campus on days you don't teach for departmental committee meetings	Usually refusing to come to campus on days you don't teach for departmental committee meetings
Willingly mentoring junior faculty, particularly new hires	Resisting mentoring junior faculty, including new hires
Attempting to secure extramural funding when it's a written or unwritten requirement for tenure and/or promotion to full professor	Resisting applying for extramural funding when it's a written or unwritten requirement for tenure and/or promotion to full professor
Not aligning yourself with a faction within your department if it's possible for you to avoid doing so	Aligning yourself with a faction within your department
Congratulating colleagues for their professional accomplishments	Ignoring colleagues' professional accomplishments

Table 1
Behaviors that at least some in your department are likely to interpret as evincing or not evincing collegiality (continued)

Evincing Collegiality	Not Evincing Collegiality
Usually offering emotional support and possibly other help (e.g., teaching a few classes) to colleagues who have experienced a personal tragedy (e.g., the death of a spouse or parent)	Rarely offering emotional support and possibly other help (e.g., teaching a few classes) to colleagues who have experienced a personal tragedy (e.g., the death of a spouse or parent)
Being sensitive to the feelings of colleagues and students when commenting on their scholarship	Being insensitive to the feelings of colleagues and students when commenting on their scholarship
Usually being willing to negotiate and compromise	Rarely being willing to negotiate and compromise
Avoiding acquiring a reputation as being someone who once his or her mind is made up "doesn't want to be confused by facts."	Acquiring a reputation as being someone who once his or her mind is made up "doesn't want to be confused by facts."
Not proselytizing colleagues or students for your religion or other deeply held moral/ethical beliefs	Proselytizing colleagues or students for your religion or other deeply held moral/ethical beliefs

your fair share of such service tasks and doing them reasonably well. Some of these are tasks that few in academia enjoy doing (e.g., attending faculty meetings). However, they are essential because almost all colleges and universities embrace some degree of "shared governance," as do most professional, academic, scientific, and scholarly organizations and many community ones.

The term *collegiality,* as it is used in academia, has two meanings. The first refers to the well-defined principle of collegial, or shared, governance. The second refers to faculty interactions with colleagues and administrators. The American Association for University Professors (AAUP) considers the first but not the second to be a legitimate area of evaluation for promotion and tenure decisions. There are items in Table 1 that relate to both meanings of the term. While I agree strongly with the AAUP's position, the fact is that both types of collegiality are considered in promotion and tenure decisions. You can protest strongly against such discrimination and make it politically (possibly even legally) incorrect to practice it overtly, but, unfortunately, it's still likely to be at least a minor consideration when making such decisions.[1]

There is a real need for you to evince both types of collegiality. You'll almost always have to cooperate with others to meet your departmental and institutional service responsibilities. That is, you'll have to function as a member of a team. Your attitude toward doing so can affect the team's ability to accomplish its mission. If you're usually perceived as being cooperative rather than combative, the team is more likely than otherwise to do so, and you're more likely than otherwise to be perceived by your peers as collegial and supported by them for tenure (continued employment) and promotion.

Judgments about collegiality are fairly subjective. They tend to be based more on abstractions (memories) and their interpretation than on facts. Consequently, it's more accurate to inquire whether your colleagues usually perceive you as evincing collegiality than whether you do so. Some behaviors are likely to enhance your image for being collegial and others are not (see Table 1).

While all faculty are expected to participate in departmental and institutional governance and exhibit collegiality in other ways, some can get away with evincing considerably less of it than can others. Your department probably will be willing to tolerate your having a weaker than usual record for collegiality/service if:

- You have an exceptional record for attracting extramural funding that's likely to continue.
- Your teaching is at least tolerable and you have an exceptionally strong reputation as a scholar.
- It would be difficult to find someone with your specialty to teach your courses and/or direct student research.
- Your institution is having financial problems or your department is attracting fewer students and your department probably won't be able to replace you if you leave.
- You are a member of a minority group that is underrepresented at your institution.
- You appear to be likely to sue the institution if you are denied tenure and/or promotion on this basis.

Attract a million dollars annually in extramural funding and you probably won't have to worry about meeting this requirement!

COLLEGIALITY ISN'T CONGENIALITY

Congeniality is behaving in a manner conducive to friendliness or pleasant social relations. While a component of your contractual obligation to your college or university is to work with fellow faculty for the accomplishment of its goals, you retain all rights of individual expression (i.e., academic freedom). In the classroom and in your publications, you have the freedom to express the truth as you see it even if your colleagues disagree strongly with your conclusions and would like to get rid of you because of them.

Collegiality is a requirement for tenure; congeniality is not. A college or university can be censured by the AAUP for denying tenure on the basis of congeniality. Furthermore, litigation against a college or university for denial of tenure on this basis, if it can be proven (i.e., if the "preponderance of evidence" indicates that a lack of congeniality was the reason), is likely to be successful.

HOW MIGHT YOU BENEFIT FROM EVINCING COLLEGIALITY?

There are a number of ways that you could benefit from evincing collegiality, including the following:

- Becoming tenured or having your contract renewed
- Being promoted
- Having more possibilities for networking
- Gaining new opportunities for research collaboration
- Being more viable for securing extramural funding
- Being invited to coauthor a text/professional/scholarly book
- Getting larger merit salary increases
- Getting nominated for offices and awards
- Not being encouraged to retire
- Having a pleasant work environment
- Friendships

Some of the reasons why evincing collegiality can enable you to benefit in these ways are indicated here.

Becoming Tenured or Having Your Contract Renewed

This is probably the most important benefit you're likely to derive from not being viewed by your colleagues as lacking in collegiality. This benefit is more likely to be a negative than a positive one. That is, the benefit is more likely to be your collegiality (service) not being questioned when you're considered for tenure or contract renewal than it is your being tenured or having your contract renewed largely because of having an outstanding record for collegiality (service). Consequently, this benefit differs significantly from those you're likely to derive from having outstanding records for research and teaching because such records are likely to facilitate your being tenured or having your contract renewed.

That said, there are a few scenarios under which an outstanding record for collegiality could be a positive for continued employment in academia. An example would be being on the faculty of a department that considers its primary mission to be undergraduate teaching. An outstanding record for doing more than a fair share of service-related tasks and being helpful to students (e.g., when advising them) would tend to be a positive for tenure and contract renewal in such a department.

Being Promoted

How others in your department view you as a colleague can affect the likelihood that you'll be promoted to either Associate Professor or Full Professor. If your bid for promotion is strongly supported by your department, you're more likely to be successful than if it isn't. Persons who are not regarded by their department as being collegial are likely to receive letters of recommendation from at least some of the faculty in their department that are equivocal. Such letters tend to be interpreted negatively by institutional promotion and tenure committees.

One way, incidentally, that departments "get even" with faculty who are considered to be severely lacking in collegiality is by not supporting them strongly when they are considered for promotion. Such a lack of support sometimes is intended to send a strong message that the person should change or leave.

Having More Possibilities for Networking

It's human nature for your colleagues to be more highly motivated to help you promote your career if they consider you to be collegial (i.e., a "team player") than if they don't. I, for example, would be more likely to volunteer to help a colleague whom I so regarded get a contract for a textbook than I would one I didn't. There are a number of ways that your colleagues, if motivated, could help to promote your career (i.e., serve as mentors), including the following:

- Nominate you for an office or for membership on a committee in your professional association
- Nominate you for an award

- Recommend that you be invited to contribute a chapter to a book or to join the editorial board of a journal
- Recommend that you be invited to participate in a conference or present a workshop
- Make it possible for you to be a coauthor on one or more of their publications
- Include you as a co-investigator or consultant on one of their grants

Some of these are dealt with elsewhere in this section.

Gaining New Opportunities for Research Collaboration

Few academics would voluntarily choose to collaborate on a research project with a colleague whom they considered unlikely to do a fair share of the work, particularly if that person wasn't somebody whose name on an article would enhance its credibility and/or likelihood of being published. A colleague who rarely evinced collegiality probably wouldn't be considered likely to do a fair share of the work in such a collaboration. Nor would such a collaboration be likely to be expected to be enjoyable. Consequently, a colleague who rarely evinces collegiality would be less likely than one who does so frequently to be invited to participate in such collaborations.

Being More Viable for Securing Extramural Funding

There are several scenarios under which your being considered collegial could increase the likelihood that you'll secure extramural funding. First, it could increase the likelihood that your colleagues would tell you about funding sources for which one or more of your projects may be viable when they "hear" about them. Second, it could increase the likelihood that a colleague in your department who had a grant would be willing to fund one of your projects from it (at least partially). Third, it could increase the likelihood that you'd be invited to collaborate with others in applying for a grant. And fourth, it would increase the likelihood that your colleagues would use whatever influence they have with those who'll be evaluating your proposal to ensure that it be given "serious consideration."

Being Invited to Coauthor a Text/Professional/Scholarly Book

For a book collaboration to stand a good chance of being successful, the coauthors have to be willing to evince considerable collegiality (e.g., do what they promise to do by when they promise to do it and be willing to negotiate to resolve disagreements). Consequently, if you usually do so in your interactions with colleagues, you're more likely to be invited to be a coauthor than if you don't.

Getting Larger Merit Salary Increases

There are at least two scenarios under which you'd receive a larger merit salary increase by evincing collegiality than you'd be likely to otherwise. The first is your receiving one, at least in part, because of having had the opportunity to collaborate with a colleague on a publication and/or an extramural funding opportunity. And the second is your being given one to discourage you from considering other job offers. Persons who teach well, are acceptable as scholars, and, in addition, usually evince collegiality in their interactions with colleagues are hard to replace!

Getting Nominated for Offices and Awards

You're more likely than otherwise to be nominated by colleagues for awards and offices in professional associations if they regard you as evincing collegiality (i.e., if they both like and respect you).

Not Being Encouraged to Retire

It's human nature for faculty to want to continue working with persons whom they like and respect (i.e., who are collegial). Consequently, being collegial can contribute to your not being encouraged to retire before you're ready to do so.

Having a Pleasant Work Environment

It's more pleasant to work in an environment in which you're liked and respected by your colleagues than in one where you aren't. Being collegial can contribute to your being liked and respected by them.

Friendships

A bonus that some academics derive from being collegial is a friendship with one or more of their colleagues. That colleagues can become friends should not be particularly surprising considering the amount of time you spend with them and the fact you share some interests.

NOTE

1. Evidence that such discrimination is practiced includes the AAUP issuing a position statement in 1999 condemning it (www.aaup.org/Redbook/S099CRpt.htm) and the American Association for the Advancement of Science in 2001 sponsoring the symposium "The Return of 'Collegiality': Scientific Careers on More or Less Than Merit?" (www.aaas.org/2001/6110.00.htm).

Chapter 2

CRITERIA USED TO EVALUATE COLLEGIALITY AND SERVICE FOR TENURE

The assessment of the adequacy of a candidate's record for collegiality and service tends to be more subjective than that for teaching or scholarship (i.e., research and publication). It's usually based largely on a phenomenon that has been referred to as *tacit knowing*. According to Polanyi (1967),

> *We can know more than we can tell.* This fact seems obvious enough; but it is not easy to say exactly what it means. Take an example. We know a person's face, and can recognize it among a thousand, indeed among a million. Yet we usually cannot tell how we recognize a face we know. (p. 4)

While your colleagues are likely to agree fairly well on whether your record for service and collegiality is adequate for them, in good conscience, to support you for tenure, they're unlikely to be able to specify all of the criteria and observations on which they based their judgment. Some of the factors that are likely to affect your colleagues' judgments, with or without their awareness, about the adequacy of your collegiality and service records for tenure are indicated in this chapter. Strategies for maximizing the likelihood that, based on these factors, they'll judge your collegiality and service records to be adequate are spelled out elsewhere in the book.

At least a few of the factors that some of your colleagues may consider when judging the adequacy of your service record for tenure aren't ones that they're supposed to consider when doing so. These tend to be ones that pertain to congeniality rather than service. Consequently, I decided to include some congeniality-related factors here. My doing so isn't intended to suggest that you should sacrifice your academic freedom in order to be perceived as congenial by your colleagues. Rather, my message is that you'd be wise to do what you can to be considered congenial by them as long as your doing so doesn't necessitate your sacrificing your academic freedom or your deeply held ethical beliefs.

The weight that an evaluator gives each factor is unlikely to be the same for all candidates. One determiner is whether he or she wants to make a case for a record being adequate or inadequate. If the former, what the person has done well will tend to be emphasized and if the latter, what the person hasn't done or hasn't done well will tend to be emphasized. Your goal should be to develop a record for service (collegiality) that's strong enough to make it extremely difficult for anyone in your department to argue cogently for it being inadequate.

The order in which factors that influence judgments about the adequacy of a service record (and, consequently, the adequacy of a record for collegiality) are discussed here is not intended to indicate the extent of their influence. Also, the factors that are mentioned in this chapter are unlikely to be the only ones that evaluators consider when making such judgments.

STUDENT ADVISING, MENTORING, AND RECRUITING

Your departmental responsibilities for students are likely to extend beyond meeting with them in a classroom or laboratory. They can include any, or all, of the following:

- Treating them appropriately (e.g., being respectful and not sexually harassing them)
- Being their academic advisor
- Being supportive (e.g., a good listener) when they have problems
- Tutoring them and otherwise being available to them as an academic resource
- Being their mentor for research and other projects
- Writing them letters of recommendation for admission to graduate school, scholarships and fellowships, and jobs
- Serving as an advisor for one of their organizations

- Attending their graduation ceremonies and other of their academic events (e.g., honors convocations)
- Being helpful to them when they become alumni
- Participating in your department's student recruitment activities

There are suggestions in Chapter 3 for maximizing the likelihood that your colleagues will conclude that you've met these responsibilities.

Failing to meet some of these student-related responsibilities is more likely to impede your being tenured than failing to meet others. Sexually harassing students would, of course, be more likely to do so than would failing to attend student convocations. Engaging in such harassment, incidentally, is highly likely to get you fired even if your research attracts millions of dollars in extramural funding and you're an excellent teacher.

MEETING COMMITTEE RESPONSIBILITIES

All colleges and universities embrace *shared governance,* to some degree, at both departmental and institutional levels. One of the main ways that faculty contribute to the governance of both their department and institution is by serving on standing and ad hoc committees. All full-time, tenure-track faculty are expected to serve on at least one (a "committee of the whole" that includes all such faculty in their department), and most will end up serving on at least three or four.

Attending committee meetings and doing other committee work can be very time-consuming. It isn't unusual for faculty to complain about the amount of time they have to invest in meeting committee responsibilities, particularly when they doubt that what their committee recommends is likely to affect the functioning of their department or institution. Regardless of whether such committees really contribute significantly to the governance of a department or institution or are merely window dressing, faculty are expected to participate. Your failing to do so conscientiously is likely to be interpreted by at least some of your colleagues as your lacking collegiality.

Most faculty, at times, wonder why they are required to spend time on tasks (such as serving on some committees) that appear to accomplish little or nothing. The need for doing so becomes at least a little more understandable when such tasks are viewed as *traditional rituals.* The academy, like religious institutions, has rituals that are traditional. One obvious one is for faculty to dress in academic attire (caps and gowns) when participating in graduation ceremonies. Another is for faculty to at least give the appearance of sharing governance. Your failure to observe certain religious rituals is likely to cause you to be ostracized by some in your religion. Likewise, your failure to observe certain academic rituals is likely to cause you to be ostracized by some in your department and/or institution because such behavior isn't considered collegial.

There is information about how to function as a committee member or chairperson to both get something done and enhance your image for being collegial in Chapter 4.

MEETING DEPARTMENTAL ADMINISTRATIVE RESPONSIBILITIES

You may at some point during your academic career be asked to take on a departmental administrative responsibility. While the ultimate such responsibility is functioning as your department's chairperson, there are others, including the following:

- Directing your department's graduate program
- Directing one or more of your department's practicum resources (e.g., clinics serving the public)
- Coordinating the teaching of a large, multisection course
- Coordinating your department's continuing education course offerings

While such administrative responsibilities usually are assumed by tenured faculty, this isn't always the case. I've even known of a few instances in which a faculty member who was not yet tenured was a department's chairperson.

Taking on a major responsibility for your department's governance can be very time consuming and is more likely to hurt, than help, your chances for being tenured, for at least three reasons. First, most departments give very little weight to performing well administratively when making tenure decisions. Second, you'll have less time to publish and do other things necessary to establish a national reputation as a scholar. And third, you may make some enemies in your department (by not giving them everything they ask for) who'll hold off getting even until you go up for tenure.

That said, suppose you're "forced" to take on some time-consuming administrative responsibilities before you're tenured. What then? My advice for such a scenario would be two-fold. First, don't assume that you'll be excused from developing a strong reputation as a scholar if you take on such responsibilities, even if someone tells you that this is so. While he or she may be willing to vote to grant you tenure without your having a strong publication record, others on your promotion and tenure committee may not. During my 30-plus years in academia, I've been acquainted with several persons who were denied tenure after being given such assurances. So if you're going to depend on them for getting tenured, get them in writing (i.e., in a letter). If the person refuses to give them to you in written form, this would say loads about their value!

My second piece of advice would be to make developing a strong reputation as a scholar a priority. You'd probably be more likely to be tenured if you did an adequate job as an administrator and some publishing than you would if you did a great job as an administrator and little or no publishing.

The alternative, of course, would be to seek a position at another college or university. It's likely to be more difficult to find a good one at the end of your probationary period than near the beginning, particularly if you have a relatively weak publication record. Deans at other institutions would probably expect to have to pay you a higher salary at the end of this period than near its beginning. Furthermore, they would tend to be more optimistic about your potential as a scholar nearer to its beginning than its end.

Information in Chapter 5 can both facilitate your performing administrative tasks efficiently and enhance your image for being collegial.

PARTICIPATING IN THE GOVERNANCE OF PROFESSIONAL ASSOCIATIONS

One aspect of collegiality that most colleges and universities highly value is the active participation of their faculty in the governance of their professional associations. Few professional associations, even large ones that have a paid staff, can accomplish their mission without such participation. The governance-related functions that faculty volunteers perform in such associations, include the following:

- Serving on one or more of standing and ad hoc committees
- Being an officer
- Serving on the Executive Council
- Editing a newsletter or journal
- Serving on the editorial board of a newsletter or journal
- Serving as webmaster for its Web site
- Planning an aspect of its annual convention

- Representing the membership of your association at meetings of an "umbrella" organization (e.g., almost all national associations for book authors send a representative to meetings of an "umbrella" organization known as the Authors' Coalition)

- Lobbying on the state or national level for the benefit of its members and possibly, also, for the population(s) they serve

A desire to serve your professional association in one of these ways usually isn't all that's necessary to be able to do so. You first have to get invited. Some strategies for getting invited and for performing assigned tasks well enough to continue doing so are presented in Chapter 8.

Having a strong record for leadership in your professional association is likely to be even more helpful for getting promoted to full professor than for being tenured and getting promoted to associate professor. One question that is almost always asked during promotion and tenure committee deliberations about candidates seeking promotion to full professor is whether they have a strong national reputation in their field. If you're seeking such promotion and you've been active for a number of years in the leadership of your national professional association, you can use this to partially document your having developed such a reputation. If you didn't have one, you wouldn't have been invited repeatedly to serve a leadership role in your professional association.

ENHANCING YOUR DEPARTMENT AND INSTITUTION'S REPUTATION

Doing things to enhance your department and institution's reputation is a great way to secure upper administrative support (e.g., that of your dean and/or your vice president for academic affairs). Such support can be particularly valuable if your department gives you only lukewarm support for tenure and/or promotion because of "personality conflicts" (e.g., ones resulting from professional envy and jealousy) or attempts to encourage you to quit or retire early by giving you less than desirable salary increases and/or more than desirable teaching loads. By enhancing your college or university's reputation, you're likely to be considered a valuable asset by your upper administration, one it would like to retain.

Enhancing your department and institution's reputation can be conceptualized as being a two-step process. The first is doing or facilitating projects that would tend to enhance the reputation of one or both if others in your profession and/or the general public knew about them. And the second is to facilitate their knowing about them. A number of strategies are described in Chapter 9 for doing the latter.

SECURING EXTRAMURAL FUNDING FOR YOUR DEPARTMENT AND INSTITUTION

Faculty who attract substantial amounts of extramural funding that at least partially pay their salary and that of at least one graduate assistant are likely to be highly valued by their chairperson, their dean, and the upper administration at their institution. One perhaps not so obvious reason for this is that their institution usually receives a percentage of the amount awarded for its overhead expenses (i.e., "indirect costs"). The amount that it receives for such expenses may exceed what it actually needs and it may be allowed to use the excess for other purposes.

It is close to impossible in some departments to be tenured or promoted if you don't have a strong record for grantsmanship, even if your teaching record is excellent and you have a strong national reputation as a scholar. Consequently, you'd be wise when interviewing for a tenure-track position to inquire about the department's expectations for grantsmanship, particularly if the research you're planning to do doesn't require extramural funding.

Some considerations and strategies for maximizing the likelihood that junior faculty will be successful at grantsmanship are presented in Chapter 6.

MEETING DEPARTMENTAL AND INSTITUTIONAL COMMUNITY RESPONSIBILITIES

Your obligations for service as a member of a college or university faculty are not limited to your institution and profession. You are also expected to use your personal and professional expertise to be helpful to persons in your community. The more your institution's community benefits from its presence, the more supportive of it they're likely to be financially and otherwise and, consequently, the less likely the institution is to experience "town-gown" conflicts.

There are a number of ways that you may be able to fulfill your obligation to help your college or university be viewed as a "good citizen" of its community, including the following:

- Volunteer to give talks to community organizations about topics in your field of expertise that would be of interest to the general public.

- Volunteer to serve on municipal and state advisory committees in your areas of professional expertise.
- Make yourself available to your local media to comment on current events.
- Be active and visible in voluntary organizations that help your community.
- Participate in a program your institution sponsors that helps persons in your community who are disadvantaged or disabled.
- Conduct classes for children in your area of expertise (e.g., art, dance, or drama).
- Conduct classes for senior citizens and others in the general public in your area of expertise (e.g., investing or writing).

These, of course, are not the only activities through which you can meet your obligation to help your institution be viewed as a good citizen of its community. Nor are they ones in which all faculty can engage. This topic is dealt with further in Chapter 7.

RELATIONSHIPS WITH COLLEAGUES AND ADMINISTRATORS

While collegiality is not supposed to be considered a component of service for promotion and tenure decisions, some in academia, consciously or unconsciously, do link the two when making them. Anybody who has been in academia for a while is likely to know of at least one instance in which the "unstated" real reason for a colleague being denied tenure or promotion to full professor was a perceived lack of collegiality.

Being considered reasonably collegial by your colleagues while you are exercising your academic freedom in ways they don't like is difficult, but not impossible. There are some suggestions in Chapter 10 for being perceived as congenial while doing so.

Chapter 3

MEETING EXPECTATIONS FOR ADVISING, MENTORING, AND RECRUITING STUDENTS

All faculty affect students' lives, sometimes profoundly, through their attempts to advise, mentor, and recruit them. The consequences of their attempts to do so, unfortunately, may not be life enhancing for students for at least three reasons:

- Their recommendations are inappropriate.
- Their recommendations are appropriate, but they are misunderstood by students.
- Their recommendations are appropriate, but ignored because students don't adequately respect or trust the person making them.

The goal to only give students recommendations that will be life enhancing for them is neither realistic nor attainable. Faculty, like all humans, are fallible. However, the goal to do what you can to *maximize the likelihood* that your recommendations to students will be life enhancing for them is both realistic and attainable. Consequently, I'll be focusing in this chapter on some things you can do to maximize the likelihood that your recommendations to students while advising, mentoring, and recruiting them will, in fact, be life enhancing.

Advising and mentoring students are viewed here as two components of the same process rather than as two separate (independent) processes. Academic advising, even of undergraduate students, involves at least a little mentoring, and mentoring of graduate students almost always involves at least a little advising.

Preparing to write this chapter was an emotionally as well as intellectually challenging experience for me. During my more than 30 years in academia, I have advised and mentored hundreds of students and tended to view doing so as being less personally rewarding than classroom teaching and research. Yet, while thinking over the amount of personal satisfaction that I've derived from advising and mentoring students over the years, I realized that what has given me the greatest professional satisfaction is having made an impact on the lives of the few students in whom I had really invested in terms of advising and/or mentoring. I very much regret not having had this insight earlier.

POTENTIAL BENEFITS AND LOSSES FROM MAKING MORE THAN A MINIMAL INVESTMENT IN ADVISING AND MENTORING STUDENTS

All faculty are expected to do some advising and mentoring of students. You'll have to decide whether to invest more in doing these activities than the minimum amount your department requires. Some of the benefits and losses that you can experience from doing so are considered here.

Potential Benefits

There are a number of ways that you'll be likely to benefit from investing more than the minimum your department requires in advising and mentoring students, including the following:

- You'll be more likely than otherwise to significantly impact the lives of your students in positive ways.
- You'll be more likely than otherwise to be loved (not just respected) by most of your students.
- Your students will be more likely than otherwise to write strong letters in support of your bid for tenure and/or promotion to full professor. (Student letters are usually a component of the application package for both.)
- You'll get to know your students as people and maybe even form long-term friendships with at least a few of them.
- If you're a "people person," you'll probably be less likely to burn out.

These are a few of the ways that you could benefit from making a larger than required investment in advising and mentoring students.

Potential Losses

Investing more in advising and mentoring students than the minimum your department requires, however, can hurt, rather than help, your career. Possible reasons include the following:

- You're likely to have less time for research and exploiting extramural funding opportunities.
- Your being loved by students can trigger professional envy and jealousy in some of your colleagues. This can cause them to give you only luke-warm support for tenure and/or promotion to full professor.

To determine whether, for you, the potential benefits from making a larger than required investment in advising and mentoring students is likely to outweigh the potential losses from doing so, you're going to have to compute this benefit-loss ratio not just once during your academic career, but repeatedly. At some points during your career the benefits may outweigh the losses and at others not.

PHILOSOPHIES OF ADVISING STUDENTS

All faculty while advising students behave in a manner consistent with a philosophy (i.e., set of assumptions) for doing so and from this philosophy they derive one or more goals. At least some faculty probably are relatively unaware that their goals while advising students are derived from such a philosophy. The goal(s) they derive from it may be limited to making certain that students are on track for meeting graduation requirements, or they may be broader.

There appear to be three basic philosophies for advising students. They are defined by the nature of the relationship that exists between the advisor and advisee. Some defining characteristics of each are indicated below.

The Prescriptive (Traditional) Philosophy

This philosophy defines the traditional relationship between an academic advisor and his or her advisees. It is based on authority and as such, it is similar to the traditional doctor-patient relationship. The advisor *prescribes* courses of action and his or her advisees are expected to follow them.

Operating from this philosophy can yield both benefits and losses for advisors and advisees. One benefit that both advisors and advisees are likely to derive from doing so is having to spend less time than they would if they utilized approaches that were based on the other two philosophies. Another benefit that advisees are likely to derive is not having to take responsibility for some of their decisions.

Perhaps the main losses that operating from this philosophy is likely to yield advisors are feelings of guilt from knowing that advising in this way is unlikely to be a positive learning experience for students because it encourages dependency, and having to place themselves at risk legally for the bad decisions that advisees make based on their advice. To minimize such legal risk, advisors should stress to their advisees that their responsibility is merely to advise: the final decision is always the student's.

The harm to students from advising based on this philosophy includes the loss of an opportunity to develop independence and to learn to make well thought out decisions. It also includes the possibility of their making poor decisions, either because they aren't aware of their options or because their advisor prescribes decisions without fully understanding their circumstances.

The Consultative Philosophy

An advisor operating from this philosophy serves as a consultant to his or her advisees. He or she attempts to make them aware of their options when they have to make a decision. The advisor may make a recommendation and give the reasons for it, but he or she does not tell the advisee what to do. Furthermore, the advisor positively reinforces advisees' attempts at making informed decisions.

Operating from this philosophy can yield both benefits and losses for advisors and advisees. One benefit that advisors are likely to derive from doing so is not having to assume responsibility for the bad decisions that advisees make based on their advice. Another is knowing that advising in this way is likely to be a positive learning experience for advisees because it encourages them to take responsibility for some of their decisions. This also is perhaps the main benefit for advisees.

One benefit that advisees are likely to derive from advising based on this philosophy is a positive learning experience. Another is a lower probability of making poor decisions because of not being aware of their options or because of their advisor prescribing decisions without fully understanding their personal circumstances.

Perhaps the main kind of loss that operating from this philosophy is likely to yield both advisors and advisees is having to spend more time than they would if an approach based on one of the other philosophies was used.

The Developmental Philosophy

The developmental philosophy contains elements of both the prescriptive philosophy and the consultative philosophy. The following excerpt from a statement that was issued by the College of Charleston Advisory Task Force (www.cofc.edu/~advising/phil.htm) contains goals that reflect this philosophy:

> Academic advising requires a commitment to assist students in taking responsibility for their own intellectual and life skills training. The steps and process of advising are therefore designed to recognize the developmental and situational needs for such assistance to students. Advising should become less intrusive, mandatory, necessary, and more collegial over time as students mature in their academic program and life skills. Effective academic advising requires the ability and willingness to make oneself available to students and colleagues for learning support purposes. It also requires familiarity with College programs, degree requirements, academic and support services, student development stages, administrative policies, and regulations related to academic performance.

ADVISING MAXIMS

The following list of principles was generated at a student advising conference at Pennsylvania State University in April 1999 (www. psu.edu/dus/mentor/000717ma.htm). You're likely to find the wisdom in at least a few of them helpful when advising students.

- The longest advising contacts usually begin with: "I have a quick question."
- Students don't know what they don't know.
- What you see is as important as what you hear.
- Universities speak a foreign language.
- Know when to challenge and when to support.
- Help students locate themselves in the university.
- Listen, then check.

- Always ask, "Why?"
- Delay assuming what the student is trying to tell you.
- You can't predict a student's fate.
- Sometimes our assumptions put students at risk.
- Just because students love courses in high school doesn't mean they will love them in college.
- The only person you can control is yourself.
- All behavior is purposeful.
- When advocating for students, when the answer is "no," it rarely is.
- Don't be afraid to give students bad news.
- Find out who "they" are (as in "well, they told me it was OK.").
- Students are not us.
- Would you want your child working with an academic advisor like you?
- Advising is a moving target.
- Students don't always provide you with all the facts or tell the absolute truth.
- Academic advising needs to incorporate the student's life-long career development needs during each session with the student.
- Students with the best ACTs or SCTs are no more mature than all other students.
- The rules change daily.
- You'll never know when you'll need to know what you know.
- The best advisors ask more questions than give answers.
- Advice is the most useless thing in the world—wise people don't need it and fools won't take it.
- Remember, everyone is in favor of progress; it's change they don't like.
- A student's present situation does not necessarily preclude a successful outcome.
- You can provide a map and directions to degree completion, but the student must be the driver and make the decisions regarding detours, stops along the way, and finishing the journey.
- Students need to be active participants in the advising process. It's a joint venture!
- Sometimes when students come looking for answers, they actually need more questions.

GOALS FOR ACADEMIC ADVISING

The National Academic Advising Association (NAAA) has proposed the following set of eight goals as a standard for academic advising (Habley, 2000, pp. 40–41):

1. Assisting students in self-understanding and self-acceptance (values clarification; understanding abilities, interests, and limitations)

2. Assisting students in considering their life goals by relating their interests, skills, abilities, and values to careers, the world of work, and the nature and purpose of higher education

3. Assisting students in developing an educational plan consistent with their life goals and objectives

4. Assisting students in developing decision-making skills

5. Providing accurate information about institutional policies, procedures, resources, and programs

6. Referring students to other institutional or community support services

7. Assisting students in evaluating or reevaluating progress toward established goals and educational plans

8. Providing information about students to the institution, college, academic departments, or some combination thereof

These goals define your responsibilities as an academic advisor. Some specific ways that you can work toward achieving them through interacting (communicating) with advisees are spelled out in the next section.

REASONS FOR STUDENTS CONSULTING A FACULTY ADVISOR

There are a number of ways that a faculty advisor can be helpful to students and, consequently, there are a number of reasons why a student might consult his or her faculty advisor. While the reasons mentioned in this section aren't the only possible ones, they do include those that students have most frequently consulted me about during the more than 25 years I've served as a faculty advisor. Be aware, however, that not all of them are a part of a faculty advisor's "scope of practice" in every department.

For further information about the ways in which a faculty advisor can be helpful to his or her advisees, see Gordon (1992) and Gordon, Habley, and Associates (2000).

To Choose a Major or a Minor

While helping students to choose a major or a minor falls within the scope of practice of all departmental faculty advisors, what such advisors usually do for students in this regard actually varies considerably. At one end of the continuum would be telling the student to read the descriptions of majors and minors in the college catalogue and when he or she has made a choice, to see the advisor to be signed up. At the other end of the continuum would be taking time to probe the student's interests, identifying a few possible majors and/or minors that might be compatible with them, and providing advice for exploring each further through Internet searches, taking introductory courses, "shadowing" persons on the job who had each, and so forth. While few academic advisors usually function at one of these extremes, I'd be willing to bet (at least a little) that those who usually function near the "high" end tend to derive considerably more satisfaction (pleasure) from academic advising than those who usually do so near the "low" one!

I'm 70 years old and have been teaching college full-time for approximately 35 years. Whenever I search my memory bank for experiences that make me feel good about having chosen a career in academia, I'm more likely to remember advising contacts with students than any of my approximately 150 journal articles or 20 books. Furthermore, the positive impact that I had on students through advising contacts is more likely to result in a few people in my field remembering me kindly 20 years after I retire or die than are my publications.

To Change a Major or Minor

A departmental faculty advisor is almost always required to have administrative involvement when his or her advisees want to change their minor but not necessarily when they want to change their major. He or she is more likely to have some administrative involvement when advisees change to another major within the department than to one outside of it.

A departmental faculty advisor can sometimes be helpful to his or her advisees in the following two additional ways when they indicate that they want to change or are considering changing their major or minor:

- Gently inquiring why they want to change or are considering changing their major or minor and offering counseling if the reason doesn't appear to have been well thought through

- Helping to facilitate their making the change if the reason does appear to have been well thought through

While doing either is usually optional, it's rarely very time consuming and is likely to give you the good kind of feeling that comes from knowing you've done something really worthwhile.

To Design a Creative and Sensible Schedule of Courses

Helping to design a student's course schedule is almost always a departmental faculty advisor's primary responsibility. The nature of an advisee's major and minor determines how time consuming doing so is likely to be. For a major like the one with which I'm involved (i.e., a professional training one that has room for only a few electives), meeting this responsibility doesn't tend to be very time consuming. However, assisting advisees in designing creative and sensible schedules of courses for majors that aren't professional or pre-professional ones can be quite time consuming if done conscientiously, particularly when their majors are interdisciplinary ones.

That said, even in a program like ours in which there is room for only a few electives, a faculty advisor's willingness to offer advice on course selection can be conceptualized as being on a continuum. At (or near) one end would be telling the advisee: "Read the course descriptions in the institution's catalog and decide." And at (or near) the other would be asking the advisee: "What are your interests, vocationally and avocationally?" The latter, of course, would be more likely than the former to yield a creative and sensible schedule of courses.

To Monitor Progress toward Meeting Degree Requirements

Monitoring students' progress toward meeting the requirements for their degree, like helping students develop a sensible schedule of courses, is one of the primary roles of departmental faculty advisors. They're required to periodically meet with their advisees and to strongly encourage them to both take the courses and maintain the GPA that they'll need to be perceived as making reasonable progress toward meeting degree requirements. For undergraduates, incidentally, it may not only involve encouraging them to maintain a high enough GPA to graduate, but also to be admitted to graduate school if the vocation to which they aspire requires graduate-level training.

If your department has a form for monitoring advisees' progress toward meeting degree requirements, then you'll certainly want to use it. However, if it doesn't have such a form, you may want to create a checklist containing all of the core and major and minor course requirements. I've been using such a form for more than 25 years. I meet with my advisees before they register for their next semester (i.e., twice a year for full-time students), enter the courses on the checklist that they're planning to take the next semester, and have them look over the entire form to make certain that there aren't courses checked on it that they didn't take or that they dropped or failed. Fortunately, thus far I haven't had to cope with a situation in which the form erroneously indicated that a student had met graduation requirements.

For Advice on Improving Grades (Study Habits)

Students who seek advice on how to improve their grades are not necessarily ones who have received low-passing or failing grades on examinations. They can also be students who have been receiving high Bs or low As and who are such perfectionists that they consider such grades unacceptable. Or they can be students who have been receiving high Bs or low As and consider them unacceptable because these grades will likely put them at a disadvantage when they apply to graduate school for admission and/or financial aid.

The advice you'd give would, of course, depend on the reason the student was seeking it. That is, if the reason was that the student was failing examinations or not doing sufficiently well on them to meet his or her goals, the advice you'd give would probably be different than if the student was doing well on exams, but not believing it because of being unrealistically perfectionistic. Being helpful when the reason is the former entails giving advice on improving study habits and/or making a referral to the institution's counseling service. And being helpful when the reason is the latter usually entails encouraging the student to seek psychological counseling to learn how to cope, at least a little better, with his or her perfectionistic tendencies. You may want to point out to such students that not learning to cope better with these tendencies is likely to significantly reduce the pleasure that they derive from anything they do, for as long as they live!

To Learn about Opportunities for Studying Abroad

Many colleges and universities offer their undergraduates the option of spending a semester abroad. Those who are contemplating doing so are likely to have questions about the implications it would have for completing degree requirements and/or about where they're considering going. As a faculty advisor, you should have available (or be able to get) the information you'll need to answer their questions about the impact that spending a semester abroad is likely to have on their completing degree requirements. For questions about where they are considering going, you're likely to have to refer them to the person on your campus who coordinates semesters abroad and/or the Web sites of the institutions they're considering. Almost all colleges and universities worldwide (even ones in developing countries) now have Web sites.

I almost always encourage students who are considering doing a semester abroad and have the necessary financial and other resources to do it. The experience of living and learning abroad can contribute significantly to both their education and their capacity to accept and respect people who view the world a little differently than they do.

For Help in Resolving a Conflict with an Instructor

Trying to help students resolve conflicts with their instructors is almost always a no-win situation for academic advisors because they're likely to get caught between their advisees and their colleagues. If they side with the student, their colleagues are likely to regard them as not being collegial. And if they side with the instructor, at least a few of their students are likely to view them as being biased.

Many, perhaps most, such conflicts can be resolved by encouraging the student to meet with the instructor with whom he or she has a conflict and attempt to negotiate a "win-win" resolution to it. Only if the student has been unable to do so and there is compelling evidence that the instructor has treated (or, worse yet, is treating) the student unfairly or unethically would it be wise for you to get involved directly, particularly if you aren't tenured yet and the instructor is a tenured colleague in your department.

If it becomes necessary for you to become involved directly, try to do it in a way that protects you and the student and, if at all possible, also the instructor. You may want to meet with the instructor and offer him or her a face-saving way to resolve the conflict. If doing this is neither possible nor successful, your next step could be to meet with the instructor's chairperson or, as a last resort, with his or her dean. If the conflict fails to get resolved at these levels and pursuing it further is likely to be fruitless, both you and the student may be forced to accept the reality that life can be unfair and sometimes the bad guys win.

Cheating or Plagiarism

There are two scenarios that could result in your seeing a student because of cheating or plagiarism. The first is that the student has been accused of cheating or plagiarism. And the second is that the student wants to report a classmate for cheating or plagiarizing.

For a student who has been accused of cheating or plagiarism and claims to be innocent, your primary responsibility will be to acquaint the student (and possibly his or her parents) with your institution's procedures for challenging the accusation. You're unlikely to be expected to help establish the student's innocence or guilt.

When a student wants to report a classmate for cheating or plagiarizing, your primary responsibility is to listen to the accusation and examine the evidence. If the evidence is compelling, you may want to alert the instructor(s) involved. I, frankly, would only alert them if the evidence were very compelling (i.e., "beyond a shadow of a doubt"). I'd rather make the error of contributing to having a student go unpunished than that of contributing to having a student punished for something he or she didn't do. Anyway, if a student gets away cheating or plagiarizing, he or she is likely to do it again and, sooner or later, to get caught red-handed.

Unfortunately, cheating and plagiarism are "fuzzy" categories (Kosko, 1993). That is, ways of behaving that are considered cheating or plagiarism in our culture are not necessarily so regarded in others. Strong students in some cultures are encouraged to help weaker ones, even to the point of helping them pass examinations. While allowing a weaker student to look at your paper during an examination would be considered reprehensible in our culture, it would be considered commendable in some others. During the mid-1990s, I was involved with a B.S. degree program in a third-world country in which we encountered and had to discourage such behavior (Silverman & Moulton, 2002).

Because of Unsatisfactory Academic Performance

In some departments, students whose academic performance (e.g., GPA) is unsatisfactory are told to make an appointment to meet with their advisor. The advisor's responsibility, at a minimum, is to make certain that such students understand the probable consequences of not improving their performance. When I see a student for this reason, I usually try to find out why the student's academic performance is unsatisfactory and make practical suggestions for improving it, if it seems at all possible to do so.

A student's academic performance can be unsatisfactory for a reason other than its not being adequate for meeting degree requirements. It may be inadequate for admission to a graduate training program for the profession to which the student aspires. If it seemed unlikely that the student could become competitive for admission to such a program, I'd attempt to help the student by pointing out other options and/or by recommending vocational counseling.

To Withdraw from a Course

One of the more frequent reasons I've been consulted by advisees has been for advice about withdrawing from a course. The student usually is either failing the course or likely to get a "C" as a final grade. I usually spell out for the student, candidly, the potential benefits and losses to him or her from dropping the course and leave the decision whether to do so to the student. I also try to be supportive to the student who has decided to drop a course, particularly if having done so adversely affected his or her self-esteem.

To Add a Course

Students in some departments need the permission of their advisor to add a course after the preregistration period. If the course will be a replacement for one that the student is considering dropping, the student should be made aware of any implications that these changes could have for meeting degree requirements.

To Change Majors

Students who want to change majors or are contemplating doing so may seek some help from their advisor. While such changes are not always voluntary (e.g., they are involuntary when a student fails to maintain the minimum GPA required for a major), they usually are. When the student doesn't have to change majors, it's necessary to find out why the student wants to do so, and if the reason does not seem to have been well thought through, to encourage the student to do so before acting. The decision, of course, is the student's to make.

To Seek Advice about Managing Conflicts with Instructors

I've occasionally had an advisee make an appointment to see me because he or she is having a "personality conflict" with an instructor. The cause in some cases is something the student has done, in others it is something the instructor has done, and in still others, both contributed significantly to the conflict.

If the conflict isn't a serious one in which the instructor appears to be at fault (e.g., sexual harassment), you'd be wise to advise the student to try to find a face-saving way for him or her and the instructor to resolve it without your becoming directly involved. If you did become involved and sided with the student, the instructor would likely view you as not being collegial. This could hurt your chances for being tenured, particularly if the instructor is a full professor in your department.

If the conflict is serious—particularly one involving the sexual harassment of a student, then I believe you're morally obligated to get involved to protect him or her. I'm currently serving as an expert witness in the litigation of such a case at another university. The litigation, in part, alleges sexual harassment of a Ph.D. candidate by her dissertation advisor. The sad thing about this case is that when the student reported the harassment to other faculty in her department, they were unwilling to get involved, even though her advisor had a reputation that made her allegation credible. It apparently hadn't occurred to them that they have an obligation to be collegial to students as well as to colleagues!

For Information about Career Interests

It isn't unusual for students to begin college before deciding on a career (i.e., major), though they may have identified the general area in which they'd like to work after graduating (e.g., health care). At least a few of your advisees are likely to seek your help for choosing a career. Your primary role will probably be alerting them to resources and strategies that could help them to do so. These could include vocational counseling, aptitude and interest testing, "shadowing" persons who work in possible areas of interest, searching the Internet for information about possible areas of interest, and/or taking introductory courses in possible areas of interest.

For Information about Major-Related Extracurricular Activities

Occasionally, an advisee may make an appointment to see you for information about an extracurricular activity that's related to their major, directly or indirectly. The activity, for example, could be a local and national organization for students having their major or an opportunity for volunteering that's related to their major. If you didn't have the information that they sought, you'd refer them to a person or source (e.g., the college catalog or Web site) where they could likely get it.

For Information about Possible Departmental Research Opportunities

An advisee may be interested in getting some research experience and may inquire about possible opportunities within the department. By identifying the student's research interests and having even a low level of awareness of the research interests and activities of your colleagues, you may be able to direct the student to one or more of them who will be able (but not necessarily willing) to provide the desired experience.

For Information about Dual Degree or Major Options

Occasionally, you may have an undergraduate advisee who is interested in exploring the possibility of having a dual major or a graduate one who is considering going for two master's degrees. Your primary role is to alert them to the requirements for and the potential benefits and losses from pursuing these options. While it is appropriate for you to make a recommendation, the decision about whether to accept it is, of course, theirs.

For Information about Preparation for Professional School

You may have undergraduate advisees who are seeking help in selecting courses for meeting admission requirements for a particular kind of professional school (e.g., medical school). They're likely to find a listing of required pre-professional courses on either the Web sites of those schools to which they'll be applying or in their catalogues.

For Internal and External Transfers

In some departments, the faculty advisor has an administrative role in facilitating an internal or external transfer. Regardless, he or she may want to meet with advisees who are requesting one to make certain that their decision has been well thought through (i.e., likely to yield more benefits than losses).

For Advice on Coping with Test Anxiety

Some students experience high levels of anxiety while taking tests that cause them to perform less well than they'd be likely to otherwise. It could affect their performance on all tests or on only certain types (e.g., true-false ones). Such anxiety is treatable. Thus, advisees who are experiencing it should be referred to the institution's counseling center or, if there is none, one in the community.

For Information about Scholarships, Assistantships, or Other Types of Financial Aid

It's not unusual for students to seek this kind of help from their advisor. To be really helpful in this way, you'll have to keep up on what's available, particularly for majors in your field. Your department might want to consider setting up and maintaining a database of financial aid opportunities for its students if it doesn't already have one.

For Disability-Related Concerns

If any of your advisees have disabilities, they may seek your advice about issues related to them that are affecting their ability to function in your department and/or elsewhere in your institution. Some may be related to what they perceive as a failure to make "reasonable accommodations" for their disability. If their concerns seem legitimate and they pertain to your department, you may want to intervene. Otherwise, you may want to recommend that the student bring his or her concerns to somebody in the office on your campus that monitors compliance with disability-related legislation.

For an International Student's Concerns

If you have advisees who aren't United States citizens, they may seek your help with problems other than the usual ones. These could include visa-related ones and problems with understanding lectures and/or reading and writing English. If there's an office on your campus that handles international students' concerns, you're probably going to want to refer them to that office for help with most problems that aren't specifically related to their major.

Choosing a Graduate Program

During the past 25 years, this has been one of the more frequent reasons for my undergraduate advisees seeking my help. All of them are majoring in either speech-language pathology or audiology and need a master's degree to be employable. The ways that I've been able to be helpful to them include the following:

- Increasing their awareness of print publications that describe and/or evaluate graduate programs in their major
- Increasing their awareness of Web sites that describe and/or evaluate graduate programs in their major
- Putting them in contact with alumni of our program who graduated from programs that they're considering
- Sharing my knowledge about programs they're considering

Undoubtedly, there are other ways that a faculty advisor could be helpful to undergraduate advisees seeking such assistance.

For Advice about Coping with Discrimination or Sexual Harassment

While neither discrimination against nor sexual harassment of students by a college or university's faculty or staff is officially tolerated, it's sometimes far from clear whether a particular act constituted discrimination or sexual harassment or whether a student's complaint about being discriminated against or being sexually harassed has merit. Both kinds of complaints have the potential to require litigation to resolve. Consequently, you'd be wise to consult with the person on your campus who handles such complaints before making recommendations. Inappropriate ones can make you sufficiently unpopular with your colleagues that they'll not support you for tenure or promotion.

For Recommendations for Graduate School, Jobs, or Financial Aid

This is a responsibility that you're almost certain to have for both your advisees and other students. It's usually an enjoyable one when you know a student well and think highly of him or her. And, of course, it's unlikely to be enjoyable when you know a student well and the student's performance has been such that you can't give him or her a positive recommendation.

The most difficult letters to write are ones for undergraduates who have been in your classes, but whom you don't know well as people. About all you know about them are the grades they have earned on exams and papers, which is also about all your colleagues know about them. They are applying for admission to graduate school, or for a job, or for financial aid and they need three letters of recommendation from faculty. Earlier in my career, I discouraged such students from asking me to write them recommendations. Later, I realized that I was hurting some students who could succeed in graduate school or at a job in their profession by doing so. So I developed a fairly general positive form letter that I could use for the purpose with only a little customizing. Obviously, such a letter won't do a student as much good as a strongly positive one from somebody who knows him or her well, but at least it can help the student to meet the recommendation letter requirement. Before agreeing to write such a letter, I do tell students that they would be better off having somebody who knows them well outside of the classroom write a recommendation.

Frequently, I've had an undergraduate advisee who I believed had the potential to be successful in graduate school or on the job in spite of having a relatively low overall GPA. The reason for the low GPA could have been one of the following:

- Goofing off during the freshman and/or sophomore year
- Working many hours a week and/or having heavy family responsibilities while attending college
- Chronic test anxiety with which the student has learned to cope
- Study skills that needed improving and that, eventually, were improved

I tend to invest more time when drafting recommendations for such students than I do for most others because they have the potential to meaningfully impact a life. That is, the recommendation can determine whether a student will be admitted to graduate school and/or get a good job.

ETHICAL CONSIDERATIONS AND
OBLIGATIONS WHEN ADVISING STUDENTS

Your obligation as a member of a college faculty to behave ethically extends beyond your teaching and scholarship. It includes your service obligations, including academic advising. Students are likely to expect their advisor to be honest, fair, loyal, and committed to excellence and decency; to respect and care for others; to keep promises; to be principled and faithful; and to be a responsible citizen (Josephson, 1988). Your institution is likely to have similar expectations for faculty functioning in this role.

Unfortunately, what constitutes ethical behavior in a particular situation isn't always clear-cut. Such ambiguous situations include those in which being viewed as behaving ethically by some people means taking one action and being viewed as behaving ethically by others means taking another. You'd be forced to deal with such a dilemma in an advising situation when doing what you thought was ethical because it benefited a student would be considered unethical by your colleagues and institution or vice versa (i.e., a situation in which you have to decide whether your primary responsibility is to behave "ethically" to your advisee or to your institution, if you can't do so to both). An example would be stating in a recommendation letter for an undergraduate advisee who has a marginal GPA and is applying to your graduate school that it underestimates his or her potential for graduate study, when you think it does but aren't certain. By making such a statement, you'd be giving a higher priority to the welfare of the student than to that of the program.

For further information about ethical considerations and obligations when advising students, see Frank (2000).

LEGAL CONSIDERATIONS WHEN ADVISING STUDENTS

Your actions while advising students can lead to litigation against you and/or your institution for a number of reasons, including breach of contract and negligence. While you can't completely protect yourself against becoming involved in such litigation, you can minimize its likelihood by functioning defensively while interacting with students.

There are a number of scenarios that could result in you and/or your institution being sued by a student or his or her parents, including the following:

- Your being accused of sexual harassment or discrimination
- Your being accused of touching a student without his or her permission (i.e., battery)
- Your failing to make an appropriate referral when you recognized that an advisee was suicidal
- Your failing to maintain confidentiality
- Your being accused of defamation (i.e., slander or libel) by an advisee
- Your failing to monitor adequately an advisee's progress toward graduation

- Your failing to recommend that an advisee change majors when the major is a pre-professional one and it becomes obvious that the student is highly unlikely to be admitted to a graduate or professional school for that profession

- Your being accused of "stealing" an advisee's research and/or intellectual property

Each of these scenarios is dealt with here.

Your Being Accused of Sexual Harassment or Discrimination

Such an accusation can destroy your career in academia in addition to involving you in litigation, possibly long term. I'm currently involved as an expert witness with a case in which a professor is alleged to have sexually harassed a student, which has been in litigation for more than 10 years.

One worthwhile piece of advice that I received at the beginning of my academic career was to keep my office door open while advising students, particularly those of the opposite sex. While the need for confidentiality occasionally outweighed this consideration, I've tried to follow it. Of course, the best defense against such accusations is avoiding doing or saying anything while with students (even in jest) that could be considered sexual harassment or discrimination.

Your Being Accused of Touching a Student without His or Her Permission (i.e., Battery)

If someone intentionally touches you without your permission (even if the contact results in no physical injury), you can sue that person for battery. The courts will protect your right to freedom from intentional and unpermitted physical contacts (Prosser, 1971).

Plaintiffs in a suit for battery do not have to prove that they were physically harmed—only that they were touched without permission. Consequently, your touching an advisee without permission could result in him or her (or his or her parents) suing you for battery. While few of your advisees are likely to even consider initiating such a suit, you should remain aware of this possibility and refrain from touching advisees, particularly ones who may be motivated to use you as a scapegoat for their academic difficulties.

Your Failing to Make an Appropriate Referral When You Recognized That an Advisee Was Suicidal

Students sometimes commit suicide. You have a moral (and possibly also a legal) responsibility to try to get an advisee who appears to you to be considering suicide some help. Even if you could suffer no legal consequences for an advisee committing suicide, imagine how you'd feel if an advisee did so after you learned that he or she was suicidal and you had done nothing to try to prevent it.

Your Failing to Maintain Confidentiality

You have an obligation to keep confidential information you receive from advisees unless you are ordered by a court to divulge it.

Your Being Accused of Defamation (i.e., Slander or Libel) by an Advisee

Slander is saying something that isn't true that hurts somebody's reputation. And libel is writing/publishing something that isn't true that does so. Doing either about an advisee can result in your being sued for defamation of character.

One scenario that can result in your being sued for defamation is your writing a negative recommendation letter for a student. According to Becker (2000, pp. 64–65):

> Defamation is a statement, either oral or written, that is damaging to the reputation of an individual and communicated to a third party. Advisors should avoid giving negative references, especially if a reference has not been solicited by the student or if there has been difficulty in the advising relationship. Such circumstances could negate the qualified immunity defense that normally exists when a reference is given in good faith and with no malicious intent, and when its contents meet a reasonable and prudent standard.

Your Failing to Monitor Adequately an Advisee's Progress toward Graduation

Part of your responsibility as an academic advisor is to monitor your advisees' progress toward graduation (i.e., their progress toward fulfilling graduation requirements). Your failure to do so as carefully as it is reasonable to expect of an academic advisor could result in you and/or your institution being sued for negligence. The reason wouldn't be that you made an error, but that you didn't function carefully enough to minimize the likelihood of making such errors. Even if your negligence didn't result in a lawsuit, it could cause sufficient trauma for your department and/or institution to make your being tenured or promoted less likely.

Your Failing to Recommend That an Advisee Change Majors When the Major Is a Pre-Professional One and It Becomes Obvious That the Student Is Highly Unlikely to Be Admitted to a Graduate or Professional School for That Profession

Your failure to recommend that an advisee change his or her major under these circumstances could precipitate a lawsuit. It would be particularly likely to do so if there was credible evidence that the reason, at least in part, was to maintain enrollment in the advisee's major.

Your Being Accused of "Stealing" an Advisee's Research and/or Intellectual Property

You're more likely to be accused of doing this by a graduate student than by an undergraduate. I'm currently involved as an expert witness in a lawsuit in which a Ph.D. candidate's advisor rejected her proposal for a dissertation and then submitted it (with only minor modifications), without either her permission or acknowledging her, to a foundation as a proposal for a fairly large research grant.

STRUCTURING AN ADVISING SESSION

When an advisee seeks your assistance, he or she is likely to either make an appointment for an advising session or drop in during your office hours. The structure outlined below is appropriate for most such sessions (Gordon, 1992, p. 53):

1. Opening the Session

   - Opening question or lead, for example, "How can I help you?"
   - Obtain student's folder or record so that relevant information is available during the session and notes can be added later
   - Openness, interest, concentrated attention are conveyed

2. Identifying the Problem

   - Ask to state the problem; help student articulate if needed
   - Help student state all relevant facts; gather as much information as needed to clarify situation for you and student

- Is presenting problem covering a real problem? Ask probing, open-ended questions
- Restate the problem in student's words; give student a chance to clarify, elaborate, or correct your interpretation, if needed

3. Identify Possible Solutions

- Ask student for his or her ideas for solving problem
- Help student generate additional or alternative solutions
- What, how, when, who will solve the problem?
- What resources are needed?
- Discuss implications for each solution if two or more are identified

4. Taking Action on the Solution

- What specific action steps need to be taken? Is procedure, information, or referral needed?
- In what order do action steps need to be taken?
- In what time frame do they need to be taken?
- What follow-up is needed? By student? By advisor?

5. Summarizing the Transaction

- Review what has transpired, including restating action steps
- Encourage future contact; make a definite appointment time if referral or assignment has been made
- Summarize what has taken place in student's folder or record including follow-up steps or assignments if made

THE MENTORING ROLE

The distinction between advising students and mentoring students is a "fuzzy" one (Kosko, 1993); the boundary between them is gray. That is, where one role ends and the other begins usually isn't clear-cut. But in general, the role is more one of advising (rather than mentoring) when students are lower-division undergraduates and more one of mentoring (rather than advising) when the students are Ph.D. candidates.

A mentor is a counselor or guide who is trusted and regarded as being knowledgeable (experienced) by those whom he or she is mentoring. The following definition, which focuses on how faculty when functioning as mentors should interact with graduate students, was developed by the Council of Graduate Schools:

> Mentors are advisors, people with career experience willing to share their knowledge; supporters, people who give emotional and moral encourage-

ment; tutors, people who give specific feedback on one's performance; masters, in the sense of employers to whom one is apprenticed; sponsors, sources of information about, and aid in obtaining opportunities; and models of identity, of the kind of person one should be to be an academic. (Zelditch, 1990)

A mentor's primary role, therefore, is to do whatever he or she can to facilitate his or her students developing their careers. Functioning in this role usually begins before students graduate and could continue for a number of years after they graduate. I've been functioning in this role for a few ex-students for more than 20 years.

There are a number of ways that a mentor can facilitate students or ex-students' careers. He or she can write them recommendations for jobs. Also, a mentor can collaborate with them on research or invite them to write chapters for books that he or she is editing. And he or she can facilitate their assuming leadership roles in their professional association(s) and can nominate them for honors. Furthermore, a mentor can counsel them when career-related decisions have to be made and when uncomfortable career-related situations have to be dealt with.

You're unlikely to be required to mentor students or ex-students. Why, then, might you want to do it? There are several ways that you could benefit from doing so. First, you could partially fulfill your religious commitment to "do unto others as you would have them do unto you." Second, you could make some long-term friendships. Third, you could receive invitations from institutions that employ them or from professional organizations to which they belong to give lectures or do workshops. And fourth, you could have as a legacy your points of view continuing to impact your field long after you retire or die. Persons who are grateful to others tend to be more likely than otherwise to accept their points of view.

There are a number of things you can do while interacting with students (particularly graduate students) that are likely to enhance your effectiveness as a mentor. Some are listed below. Almost all are based on comments in an online mentoring manual by Earl Lewis, Dean of the Horace H. Rackham School of Graduate Studies at the University of Michigan (www.rackham.umich.edu/StudentInfo/Publications/FacultyMentoring/Fmentor.pdf).

The following are some ways to enhance your effectiveness as a mentor:

- Spend time talking informally with the students you mentor at least once a semester and show an interest in them as people. Your doing so lets them know that you both value and respect them. Graduate students need such validation!

- Demystify graduate school. Clarify your program's expectations. Answer questions about your program in a way that doesn't make students feel foolish for asking them.

- Provide students with forthright assessments of their work in a compassionate way and timely manner. Criticism should be constructive and praise should be given when it is deserved.

- Provide encouragement and support. Engage continuously in promoting (facilitating) the professional growth of the students you're mentoring. Encourage them to develop professionally to a level that exceeds the one they thought they were capable of attaining.

- Help foster networks. If you cannot provide something that a student needs, suggest other people who might be of assistance.

- Be an advocate for students you're mentoring both in and outside of your department (including local and national professional associations) and let them know up front that you want them to succeed.

- Treat students you're mentoring with respect. For example, give them your full attention while you're talking with them.

- Provide a personal touch. Be open and approachable when students you mentor have a need to discuss academic and nonacademic issues that arise while they are in graduate school. Let them know that you care about them as people.

THE RECRUITING ROLE

You're likely to be regarded by your colleagues as having a responsibility to your department/program to be both proactive and reactive in recruiting students for it. There can be several reasons, the most compelling of which could be *survival*. Colleges and universities, like almost all institutions in our society, have become very bottom-line oriented. Departments/programs are expected to attract funding sufficient to at least come close to paying their own way. Consequently, those that fail to attract adequate numbers of students are unlikely to generate adequate amounts of tuition to support themselves, thereby placing themselves "at risk" for losing faculty lines or, worse yet, being terminated. Loss of faculty lines (positions) for this reason is quite common and the termination of programs because they no longer attract adequate numbers of students isn't a highly unusual event.

Another reason why faculty are expected to be both proactive and reactive in recruiting students, particularly graduate students, is the desire to attract high-quality ones—that is, students who are likely to be intellectually stimulating for faculty to teach and collaborate with on research as well as reflect well on the program after they graduate.

There are a number of ways that faculty can contribute to student recruitment, including the following:

- Present "career day" talks about your profession at middle schools and high schools.
- Encourage and facilitate interested middle school and high school students to "shadow" persons working in your field.
- Give tours of your facilities to middle school and high school students who express an interest in your field (possibly through their guidance counselors) and their parents and otherwise make yourself available to them to answer questions about your program and profession.
- Participate in student recruitment "open houses" sponsored by your department or college.
- Personally respond to inquiries about your program from students, particularly potential graduate students. Offer to be helpful to them in any way that you can.
- Conduct community outreach for your program using newspapers, radio, television, and/or presentations at community-based organization meetings.
- Identify potential students (e.g., from local science fairs) and inform them about your program and profession.
- Conduct summer workshops for middle school or high school students who are interested in learning about your profession.

Chapter 4

COPING WITH COMMITTEE RESPONSIBILITIES

One service-related responsibility that few, if any, in academia can escape completely is serving on committees, which exist at departmental, college, and institutional levels. They also exist in almost all of the scientific and professional associations to which academics belong and in some community-based organizations, participation in whose committees are encouraged by institutions.

These responsibilities arise from the principle that governance of academic institutions and scientific and professional associations should be both shared and "bottom-up" rather than "top-down." Policy for the governance of an academic institution is supposed to be determined mainly by its faculty (or their representatives), not by its upper administration. And policy for the governance of a scientific or professional association is supposed to be determined mainly by its members (or their representatives), not by its president or its paid administrators. However, like many things in life, what's supposed to happen and what does happen are not necessarily the same.

HOW MEETING COMMITTEE RESPONSIBILITIES CAN AFFECT PROMOTION AND TENURE DECISIONS

Judgment about a candidate's contributions to committees is more likely to be a negative than a positive in promotion and tenure decisions. A relatively strong record for meeting committee responsibilities is highly unlikely to outweigh a relatively weak one for publication or grantsmanship. That said, most academics and administrators view committee work as a necessary evil and would be reluctant to tenure someone who isn't willing to do his or her fair share of it, unless that person has an absolutely outstanding record for publication and/ or grantsmanship. Even then, they may be reluctant to tenure the person, because others would have to do more than their fair share of it (i.e., they would have to pick up the slack). Therefore, not doing your fair share of committee work can reduce the likelihood that you'll be tenured.

But doing far more than your fair share of committee work can also be a negative for being tenured, particularly if it was done voluntarily and you have a relatively weak record for publication and/or grantsmanship. The reason is that your colleagues may consider it to have been a strategy for avoiding responsibilities they value more highly (e.g., publication and grantsmanship).

Doing one's fair share of committee work, incidentally, remains a consideration for promotion from associate professor to full professor. A person who is viewed by colleagues as not doing a fair share of committee work may be "punished" by not having his or her bid for promotion to full professor supported.

Continuing to do one's fair share of committee work is also a consideration in a department's decision about whether to encourage a tenured faculty member to retire. A faculty member who has ceased doing a fair share of committee work is more likely to be encouraged to retire than one who hasn't. While tenured faculty can continue to teach regardless of how they're viewed by colleagues, few would choose to do so if the environment in which they'd have to function was a very hostile one.

ACADEMICS' RESERVATIONS ABOUT THEIR COMMITTEE RESPONSIBILITIES

Few academics (with the possible exception of those who are full-time administrators) consider serving on committees to be one of their most worthwhile work-related activities. They may, in fact, strongly resent having to do so for a number of reasons, including one or more of the following:

- Doing so consumes time they'd prefer to invest in activities that are given greater weight in tenure and promotion decisions, such as research, writing for publication, and grantsmanship.

- Doing so consumes time they'd prefer to invest in activities that they consider more important and/or rewarding, such as research and writing for publication.

- They believe that much of the time that they spend on committee responsibilities (attending meetings and writing reports) is wasted—that is, it doesn't contribute to achieving a goal that's consistent with the committee's mission.

- They believe that the committee's recommendations, even if they're potentially helpful, are unlikely to be given serious consideration when decisions are made for which they're relevant.

- They believe that standing committees to which they're assigned have no real mission when they're assigned to them.

- They feel that their contributions aren't valued by other committee members.

Some possible reasons for these attitudes are indicated below.

Doing So Consumes Time They'd Prefer to Invest in Activities That Are Given Greater Weight in Tenure and Promotion Decisions

Meeting departmental expectations for committee work is considerably less likely to enhance one's chances for promotion and tenure than is meeting departmental expectations for research, publication, and grantsmanship. Consequently, it's not particularly surprising that many academics would prefer to spend their time "on the job" when they aren't involved with teaching on research, publication, and/or grantsmanship than on committee work.

While doing one's fair share of committee work is unlikely to significantly enhance one's chances for promotion and tenure, not doing it can significantly reduce one's chances for achieving both. Not doing one's fair share is likely to be interpreted as evincing a lack of collegiality (i.e., not being a team player). While you're unlikely to be denied promotion or tenure on this basis, it can result in your teaching, research, publication, and grantsmanship records being scrutinized far more carefully than they would otherwise. One reason why your colleagues may be angered by your not doing your fair share of committee work is that one or more of them will have to pick up the slack.

Doing So Consumes Time They'd Prefer to Invest in Activities That They Consider More Important and/or Rewarding

More people are probably attracted to a career in academia because of the opportunities it provides to do research and write for publication than are attracted to one because of the opportunities it provides to serve on committees. Yet, if you were to ask persons who have been in academia for more than 25 years to indicate from which of their contributions they derive the greatest personal satisfaction, many (including me) would probably mention ones that resulted, directly or indirectly, from serving on committees. Personal fame, though nice, wears thin. Long-term satisfaction comes from helping others.

They Believe That Much of the Time That They Spend on Committee Responsibilities (Attending Meetings and Writing Reports) Is Wasted

Spending time on committee responsibilities that don't actually contribute to accomplishing the committee's mission is something I've experienced a number of times during my 35 years in academia. The reason usually was either that the committee lacked a clearly stated, attainable mission (or missions) or the chairperson didn't facilitate achieving its mission in a direct, straightforward, well-organized manner. For example, much time was spent at meetings talking about things that weren't relevant to the committee's mission.

That said, perhaps it is worthwhile to spend time at committee meetings talking about things that aren't directly related to its mission. Committee meetings may be the only opportunity that some faculty have to interact with each other. The networking that could result has the potential to yield significant benefits for students, the faculty involved, and/or the institution.

They Believe That the Committee's Recommendations, Even If They're Potentially Helpful, Are Unlikely to Be Given Serious Consideration

I've served on committees that were either intended to rubber-stamp what had already been decided or had a mission that, if accomplished, would be highly unlikely to impact on anything. I've demonstrated a willingness to be collegial by serving on them, but have restricted my time and energy investments in them to the absolute minimum possible.

They Believe That Standing Committees to Which They're Assigned Have No Real Mission When They're Assigned to Them

A chairperson of a standing committee may schedule meetings even if the committee has no real mission at the time. I, like most faculty, deeply resent having to attend such meetings (particularly if refreshments aren't served).

They Feel That Their Contributions Aren't Valued by Other Committee Members

Many times when I've commented at committee meetings, I've felt that my opinions weren't valued by other committee members, particularly when they didn't agree with those of the majority of members present. And many times at committee meetings when opinions were expressed that differed from mine, I didn't value them either. This is normal behavior for human beings and though exasperating at times, has to be tolerated.

ATTITUDE IS EVERYTHING, ALMOST!

How much you enjoy serving on committees is determined as much (perhaps more) by how you evaluate the experience as it is by the experience itself. As Albert Einstein is reported to have commented, the world as we know it is a product of "the observer and the observed." What we abstract from an event and the interpretation we give it determines, in large part, our reaction to (evaluation of) that event. The "filter" through which we view an event determines both what we abstract from it and the interpretation we give to what we abstract from it. Consequently, two persons viewing an event through different filters are likely to evaluate that event differently.

Whether you evaluate serving on a committee positively or negatively will be determined, in large part, by the components of the filter through which you view the experience. These components can include any or all of the following:

- Your previous experiences serving on committees
- Your expectations for serving on this committee
- Your location on the optimistic/pessimistic continuum

- The extent to which your orientation when evaluating is multivalued
- Your other responsibilities

Some of the ways that each of these five filter components can affect your attitude toward serving on committees are spelled out below. Hopefully, by becoming more cognizant of them, you'll be better able to develop a fairly positive attitude toward having this responsibility. It's one that you'll probably be unable to avoid, so you may as well make having it as enjoyable as you can for yourself!

Your Previous Experiences Serving on Committees

People tend to expect situations (events) to replicate themselves and, therefore, they're likely to filter similar, new situations in ways that tend to support their expectations. That is, they tend to abstract (pay attention to) aspects of them that are consistent with their expectations and ignore those that aren't. Thus, such expectations can become a self-fulfilling prophecy.

It shouldn't be surprising, therefore, that those who have mostly unpleasant memories of serving on committees are likely to expect subsequent such experiences to be unpleasant as well. And having such an expectation, they'll usually have little difficulty finding things to confirm it. If, on the other hand, they don't expect the experience to replicate itself (i.e., they don't anticipate serving on the committee being unpleasant), their evaluation of the experience after doing it could be different.

Your Expectations for Serving on This Committee

The first time you served on a committee, you probably had some expectations about how much you'd enjoy the experience. You're likely to have expectations about this whenever you're appointed to a committee, and these expectations probably won't be based completely on your previous experiences serving on committees. There are a number of reasons why you could look forward to serving on a particular committee, including one or more of the following:

- You have a strong interest in its mission.
- You respect the chairperson and the other committee members.
- Serving on it enhances your status at your institution and/or in your profession.
- Serving on it provides opportunities for networking.
- Serving on it is intellectually stimulating.

- Serving on it provides opportunities for travel.
- Members socialize in enjoyable ways.
- Refreshments or meals are served at meetings.

On the other hand, there are a number of reasons why you may not look forward to serving on a particular committee, including one or more of the following:

- You have no interest in its mission.
- You don't get along well with its chairperson or with one or more of its members.
- Meetings probably will be scheduled too frequently or at times that are inconvenient for you.
- Meetings are unlikely to be well organized and, consequently, much of the time at them is likely to be wasted.
- No coffee or other refreshments will be served at meetings.

Your Location on the Optimistic/Pessimistic Continuum

Usually, the closer you are to the optimistic (positive) end of this continuum, the more likely you are to enjoy serving on a committee. The reason is that you're likely to attend more to (i.e., abstract) aspects of the experience you consider positive than to those you consider negative. And, furthermore, you're likely to give more weight when evaluating the experience to the positive things that happened to you than to the negative ones.

Your expectations about serving on a particular committee can be affected by comments by persons who are serving or have served on it. If their evaluation of the experience tends to be negative, one possible reason is that their orientation toward life tends to be at the pessimistic (negative) end of this continuum. Such persons tend to focus more on the negative than the positive when evaluating an experience.

The Extent to Which Your Orientation When Evaluating Is Multivalued

Persons who are perfectionistic (i.e., have a two-valued orientation) are more likely to evaluate an experience, such as serving on a committee, negatively than are those whose orientation tends to be multivalued (Johnson, 1946). Consequently, they are less likely to enjoy what they experience. Persons who have a multivalued orientation can enjoy something that isn't perfect.

Your Other Responsibilities

Your expectations regarding the impact that serving on a committee is likely to have on your ability to meet your other responsibilities (particularly ones you value more) will obviously affect your attitude toward serving on it. The greater the impact you anticipate from doing so, the more unpleasant you're likely to deem the experience.

AN ACADEMIC COMMITTEE IS A TEAM WHOSE MISSION IS PROBLEM SOLVING

Academic committees can be classified in a number of ways. I believe that one of the most useful for both understanding and facilitating their functioning is classifying them as *teams*. By doing so, we can tap into a large body of information about what makes teams function poorly and well (e.g., see Lundy, 1994 for an overview).

All teams have goals. And the goal that most (if not all) academic committees should have is to, directly or indirectly, help to solve one or more problems. When academic committees do so directly, their votes determine policy. And when they do so indirectly, their recommendations advise those who determine policy. A departmental promotion and tenure committee would be an example of an academic committee whose recommendations are advisory: they are utilized by the institutional promotion and tenure committee and/or the person(s) in the upper administration whose responsibilities include making promotion and tenure decisions.

The mission of an academic committee, incidentally, may be merely to exist. Departments at your institution, for example, may be required by upper administration to have a particular committee even though, for your department, it isn't relevant. Your chairperson may consider it more expedient to establish the committee than to try to convince upper administration of this.

ATTRIBUTES OF ACADEMIC COMMITTEES

Academic committees differ from each other in a number of ways, including the following:

- Their mission
- Whether they are standing committees or ad hoc committees

- The scope of their "territory"
- How they communicate and conduct business
- How often they meet
- The extent to which their recommendations are advisory
- The extent to which their agenda and recommendations are controlled by persons who aren't members
- The extent to which they conduct their business in "executive sessions"
- The manner in which they publish their recommendations
- The manner in which their minutes are recorded and disseminated
- The manner in which their chairperson and members are selected
- The length of appointments to them
- Their position in the hierarchy of similar committees
- The extent to which their chairperson's functioning is authoritarian
- The consequences for missing meetings
- Whether food is permitted or provided at meetings

Some practical implications of each are spelled out below.

Their Mission

Academic committees, of course, have different missions. Some (e.g., promotion and tenure committees) tend to be more sharply focused than others (e.g., curriculum committees).

Whether They Are Standing Committees or Ad Hoc Committees

Standing committees are ones that departments, colleges, universities, associations, and communities always have. They exist even when there is no work for them to do. Departments, for example, may have a promotion and tenure committee even during academic years when no one in the department is going up for promotion or tenure.

Ad hoc committees are established to accomplish a specific mission and are usually disbanded after the mission has been accomplished. The mission is usually one that either can't or isn't convenient to have done by a standing committee. Members of the existing standing committees, for example, may lack the expertise needed to accomplish the mission.

The Scope of Their "Territory"

Academic committees differ with regard to the numbers of persons that their recommendations are likely to affect directly. The decisions of some impact on the lives of more persons than do those of others. At one end of the continuum would be a committee for a master's thesis whose decisions would only impact directly on the lives of two persons—the student and his or her thesis advisor. At the other end of the continuum would be the legislative council of a large professional/scientific association (e.g., the American Speech-Language-Hearing Association, which has more than 100,000 members) whose decisions would impact directly on the lives of all its members.

How They Communicate and Conduct Business

Members of academic committees have traditionally communicated with each other and conducted business mostly during formal meetings. However, because of the substantial time and financial investments that may be required to do this, the members of some committees (particularly ones for national academic associations) now communicate and conduct much of their business by e-mail and conference calls.

How Often They Meet

Some academic committees schedule meetings in advance at set intervals (e.g., twice a month or twice a year) and others on an "as needed" basis. The former tend to meet more often than the latter.

The Extent to Which Their Recommendations Are Advisory

The recommendations of some committees establish policy and those of others offer data and/or advice to those who do so. The report of a departmental promotion and tenure committee, for example, offers data and advice to members of the institutional promotion and tenure committee and to persons in the upper administration who are responsible for making promotion and tenure decisions.

The Extent to Which Their Agenda and Recommendations Are Controlled by Persons Who Aren't Members

Constraints are placed (directly or indirectly) on the agenda and possible recommendations of some committees by persons who aren't members of it (e.g., department chairpersons or deans). The actual mission of a committee, in fact, may be to rubber-stamp what has already been decided.

The Extent to Which They Conduct Their Business in "Executive Sessions"

Persons who aren't members of committees are usually allowed to attend their meetings as observers. However, when a committee goes into *executive session,* only its members are allowed to be present. This usually happens when information is to be dealt with that the committee's chairperson considers confidential. Committees vary considerably with regard to how often they go into executive session.

The Manner in Which They Publish Their Recommendations

The manner of publication can range from an oral report at a meeting or a memorandum to a relatively long report that's published in a journal or as a book. For institutional academic committees, the former is far more common than the latter.

The Manner in Which Their Minutes Are Recorded and Disseminated

Minutes may be prepared from notes taken at committee meetings or from tape recordings of them. The person responsible for doing the minutes may be a secretary or a member of the committee. If it is the latter, the same committee member may do them for every meeting or committee members may take turns doing them.

Traditionally, minutes of committee meetings have been circulated in printed form. Now, however, they are sometimes disseminated by e-mail and/or by being posted on a Web site.

The Manner in Which Their Chairperson and Members Are Selected

There are three ways that persons are selected to serve on academic committees. The first is by being appointed by someone (e.g., their department's chairperson or the chairperson of the committee). The second is by volunteering. And the third is by being elected (members of university committees on faculty are usually selected in this way).

Chairpersons are selected in one of two ways. The first is by being appointed by someone (e.g., a chairperson). And the second is by being elected by the other members of the committee.

The Length of Appointments to Them

An appointment to an ad hoc committee is usually for the length of time it takes for the committee to accomplish its mission. An appointment to a standing committee is usually for between one and three years. However, it can be for considerably longer. I've been serving on one for more than 10 years.

Their Position in the Hierarchy of Similar Committees

The recommendations of some committees are given greater weight in decision making than those of others. For example, upper administration is likely to give more weight to the recommendations of the college or university's promotion and tenure committee when making a decision about a candidate than they are to those of his or her department's promotion and tenure committee.

The Extent to Which Their Chairperson's Functioning Is Authoritarian

The chairpersons of some academic committees function in a more authoritarian manner than do others. In some cases, their functioning is so authoritarian that the committee's recommendations and decisions are, for the most part, the recommendations and decisions of the chairperson. That is, the opinions of other committee members have little impact.

That said, the reality is that a chairperson of a committee sometimes has to function in an authoritarian manner if the committee is to accomplish its mission. The usual reason is that most, if not all, of the other committee members are unwilling to invest the time and energy necessary to contribute to formulating reasonable recommendations and decisions.

The Consequences for Missing Meetings

Chairpersons of academic committees vary somewhat in the importance they place on committee members attending meetings and doing their homework. Most get upset if a committee member continually misses meetings and/or doesn't prepare adequately for them. They may get even with the slacker in the letter they write for his or her dossier when the person goes up for tenure and/or promotion, by interpreting the lack of participation as a lack of collegiality.

Whether Food Is Permitted or Provided at Meetings

There's considerable anecdotal evidence that indicates that people tend to enjoy and participate more fully in committee meetings when coffee, soft drinks, and other light refreshments are available. This is particularly true for meetings that are scheduled immediately before or during their usual mealtimes. There's also anecdotal evidence that indicates they're more likely to enjoy and participate in committee meetings that are scheduled during their usual lunchtime if the chairperson encourages them to bring their lunch.

REPRESENTATIVE STANDING COMMITTEES IN WHICH ACADEMICS ARE PARTICIPANTS

Academics serve on a wide variety of standing committees. Some are attached to their institution; others, to their scholarly/professional associations; and still others, to their community. Some committees are called by a different name (e.g., "council").

The committees that are mentioned in this section are only a small sample of those on which persons in academia serve. I tried to select ones that exist in most institutions, organizations, and communities.

Departmental Standing Committees

There are a number of standing committees that exist in many college and university departments, including the following:

- **The faculty.** The faculty of a department usually isn't thought of as being a committee. However, departmental faculty meetings are, in reality, meetings of a committee of the whole. The deliberations that occur at them yield recommendations and decisions for solving problems.
- **Executive committee.** This committee usually consists of all tenured faculty in the department. It establishes department policy for a wide range of issues.
- **Promotion and tenure committee.** This committee does an initial evaluation of the dossiers of faculty who are going up for tenure and/or promotion. A report giving their recommendation and the rationale for it is added to each such dossier.

- **Faculty development committee.** The primary mission of this committee is to mentor junior faculty in ways that will facilitate their developing a record for teaching, scholarship, grantsmanship, and service that's adequate for being tenured.

- **Curriculum committee.** Its mission is to constantly scrutinize the undergraduate and graduate curricula to ensure that they both continue to reflect the "scope of practice" of practitioners in the field and meet institutional, state, and/or national program accreditation requirements.

University College Standing Committees

There are standing committees that exist in at least a few colleges at almost all universities. They include the following:

- **Executive committee.** A representative from each department in the college (usually the chairperson) serves on it. Its mission is to make recommendations to the dean about issues that affect the entire college. The dean may attend its meetings.

- **Promotion and tenure committee.** Usually one tenured member of the faculty of each department serves on it. It evaluates the dossiers of faculty within the college who are going up for tenure and/or promotion. A report containing its vote and the reasons for it is added to the candidate's dossier. It may also do three- or four-year reviews of the progress of junior faculty toward achieving tenure.

- **Faculty development committee.** The primary mission of this committee is to mentor college faculty (particularly junior faculty) so that they'll become more effective as teachers and scholars. It may, for example, sponsor workshops on distance teaching, writing academic books, or grant writing.

Institutional Standing Committees

There are standing committees that exist at almost all universities. They include the following:

- **Promotion and tenure committee.** This is usually the final committee that evaluates the dossiers of faculty who are seeking tenure and/or promotion. Its votes are usually given considerable weight by the persons in the institution's administration who are responsible for making such decisions.

- **Committee on faculty.** The mission of this committee is to promote faculty welfare. It deals with issues that affect all faculty (e.g., salaries).

There ordinarily is one representative from each college, who's usually elected.

- **Institutional review board.** The mission of this committee is to evaluate all research being done at the institution that utilizes human subjects to ensure either that the subjects are not placing themselves at risk for being harmed or if they are placing themselves at such risk, that they will be giving their informed consent to do so.

- **Board of Graduate Studies.** The primary mission of this committee is to periodically evaluate existing graduate programs and proposals for new ones. Its recommendations advise both the dean of the graduate college and the upper administration (including the president and the board of trustees).

Organizational Standing Committees

There is at least one standing committee in all of the associations to which academics belong. This committee is likely to be referred to as the executive council, the executive board, or the legislative council. Its membership may include the officers of the association, in addition to persons who have been elected to serve on it by the membership. Its primary role is to oversee the functioning of the association—that is, facilitate its accomplishing its mission. Such an association may also have other standing committees, such as a publications board.

Community Standing Committees

Academics serve on the councils of a number of nongovernmental organizations and municipal and state administrative agencies. I, for example, have been serving on the Governor's Advisory Council for Wisconsin's Telecommunication Relay Service for more than 10 years.

FACILITATING THE FUNCTIONING OF AN ACADEMIC COMMITTEE

There are a number of things the chairperson of an academic committee and/or its members can do to increase the likelihood that the committee will accomplish its mission. Some of these are presented here. Much of the following material was paraphrased from Lundy (1994).

The characteristics of an academic committee that's likely to accomplish its mission include the following:

- Meetings are planned with care.
- An agenda is distributed to members prior to the meeting.

- The meeting is conducted as specified in the agenda.
- There is follow-up on action commitments.
- There is continual review of meeting effectiveness and efficiency.

Some of what's needed to achieve each of these goals is indicated below.

Meetings Are Planned with Care

It's crucial that the mission the committee is expected to accomplish at its meetings be both sharply defined and doable. If the mission isn't defined sharply, holding meetings before it is so can be a waste of time, unless, of course, the purpose of the meetings is to define the committee's mission. A newly appointed chairperson of a departmental standing committee that has no real mission at the time may be motivated to schedule a meeting merely to communicate that he or she is taking the responsibility seriously. Such a meeting is not only likely to be a waste of time for its members, but it's also likely to reinforce any negative feeling they have about serving on the committee.

Attempting to accomplish a mission that isn't doable at the time can yield both frustration and resentment for committee members. Several times while I've been on a committee, the information we needed to sharply define a mission wasn't available and, consequently, the mission could not be accomplished. It would have made more sense for us to have delayed deliberating on the mission.

Chairpersons of committees should ask themselves before scheduling a meeting whether there's a more efficient way to accomplish their goal. Could it be accomplished more efficiently by e-mail or by individual or conference telephone calls? Or could it be accomplished more efficiently by a combination of one or more of these and meetings rather than by meetings only? If a meeting would be the most efficient way to accomplish a goal, then that is the way it should be done. However, if there's a more efficient way, then *that* is the way it should be done.

An Agenda Is Distributed to Members Prior to the Meeting

This should indicate both what issues will be dealt with at the meeting and what committee members should read and/or do to prepare for the meeting. The more sharply these issues are defined in the agenda, the more likely it is that committee members will give them some serious thought before the meeting and, consequently, the more likely it is that there will be some progress toward resolving them at the meeting.

The agenda should also indicate, of course, the date of the meeting, where it's being held, and the beginning and ending times. If beverages and/or other refreshments are being served, you may want to state this: it could result in at least one member's attitude toward attending the meeting being a little more positive than it would be otherwise.

The Meeting Is Conducted As Specified in the Agenda

Meetings should begin and end on time and the issues dealt with should be those specified in the agenda. About the only deviation from an agenda that's likely to be appreciated by almost all committee members is a meeting ending earlier than specified because the necessary business was transacted quicker than expected.

A well-known, three-step formula for structuring lectures—"tell them what you're going to tell them, tell them, and tell them what you told them"—with a little modification, is also applicable to structuring committee meetings. The first step would be for the chairperson of the committee to briefly review the purpose of the meeting, present an overview of the agenda, and indicate any changes that were made in it. He or she might also make some announcements, clarify relevant background and procedures, and/or review progress on prior goals and commitments.

The second step would be for the members of the committee to discuss each item on the agenda as briefly as appropriate. Goals and action steps should be clarified after each item is discussed (Should we vote now? If no, what action? By whom? When?). The votes, goals, and action commitments should be indicated in the minutes.

The third step would be for the chairperson of the committee to summarize what was decided and review the action commitments. He or she may also schedule future meetings or conference calls at this time.

There Is Follow-Up on Action Commitments

For an academic committee to accomplish its mission, much of its work is likely to have to be done between meetings, because this is when members will be expected to meet their action commitments. Minutes of the meeting should be distributed as soon as possible after it to remind members of their commitments. They should be encouraged to communicate with the chairperson periodically to inform him or her about their progress toward meeting them. If the chairperson doesn't hear anything from a committee member about a commitment after the deadline for meeting it has passed, he or she should "respectfully" inquire about its status. If it appears unlikely that the member will be able to meet the commitment, it should be assigned to another committee member, preferably not the chairperson.

There Is Continual Review of Meeting Effectiveness and Efficiency

A committee meeting is a process (methodology) for accomplishing a mission. And like all processes, it's desirable for it to be as effective and efficient as possible. The only way that the effectiveness and efficiency of this process can be improved is to continually evaluate it and make necessary modifications. To facilitate doing this, the chairperson should ask himself or herself after each meeting how it went and what he or she can do to make future meetings go better. And, in addition, periodically (perhaps every fourth or fifth meeting) ask committee members to provide feedback and discuss their perceptions of how the meetings are going.

Part of this review should be to question whether further meetings are really necessary. It isn't unusual for committees to continue meeting regularly beyond the point that doing so facilitates accomplishing their mission.

Chapter 5

COPING WITH ADMINISTRATIVE RESPONSIBILITIES

Few in academia who have tenure-track positions have training in administration. And even fewer in academia sought such a position because they wanted to be an administrator. Most did so because they wanted to teach and/or do research. Yet most tenure-track faculty have to cope with having administrative responsibilities sometime during their academic career. They may become the chairperson of their department, a chairperson of a committee, or an officer in a professional, scientific, or scholarly association. Coping successfully with these responsibilities requires certain knowledge and skills. Some of these are indicated in this chapter.

SHOULD YOU BE A DICTATOR OR A FACILITATOR?

Whenever you take on an administrative responsibility, you have to decide whether your role should be that of a dictator or a facilitator. While very few persons in academia are likely to view themselves as being dictators when meeting their administrative responsibilities, many are perceived as such by those whose activities they administer.

The bottom line for any administrator is to accomplish certain objectives. They, of course, will be different for the CEO of a large corporation and the chairperson of a departmental committee. Yet, the characteristics of leadership that maximize the likelihood of accomplishing them are the same for both. Consequently, persons in academia who want to be able to cope more effectively with their administrative responsibilities can benefit from studying relevant business administration literature. Much of the information in this chapter is from this literature.

Any manner of functioning in a leadership role can yield both benefits and losses. Perhaps, the most sensible way to decide on a leadership style is to compute a benefit/loss ratio for the alternatives. We'll consider some potential benefits and losses for an academic in this section from leading as a dictator and a facilitator. Hopefully, they'll be helpful to you when selecting a leadership style.

Potential Benefits from Leading As a Dictator

The fundamental principle underlying the dictator leadership style is that "might makes right." The leader is in a stronger position than the group's members and, consequently, the leader can impose his or her will on them. The potential benefits to a leader from functioning in this way include the following:

- The decisions and action recommendations of the group will be his or hers.
- Decisions and action recommendations will tend to be made more rapidly because the group, at most, will usually just rubber-stamp what the leader has decided.

Potential Losses from Leading As a Dictator

Leading a group as a dictator also has the potential to yield losses, including the following:

- The members of the group probably will deeply resent your doing so for a number of reasons, including violating a sacred doctrine of academia—shared governance.
- The members of the group will be less likely than otherwise to be highly motivated to invest themselves in (buy into) achieving its mission.
- You'll be placing your group at greater risk than otherwise for making a bad decision or recommendation.
- You'll have to assume full responsibility for your group's bad decisions and recommendations.

Potential Benefits from Leading As a Facilitator

The fundamental principle underlying the facilitator leadership style is that the leader does whatever is necessary to motivate the group to accomplish its mission. The leader functions like the coach of a winning basketball team. That is, he or she *motivates* the members of the team (group) to enthusiastically help the team achieve its goal. The potential benefits to a leader from functioning in this way include the following:

- The members of the group will be more likely than otherwise to buy into (feel ownership of) its mission.
- The members of the group will be more likely than otherwise to do what's necessary for the group to accomplish its mission.
- The members of the group will be more likely than otherwise to respect the leader and consider his or her interactions with them to be collegial.
- The group will be at less risk than otherwise for making a bad recommendation or decision.
- The leader will not have to assume full responsibility for bad recommendations and decisions.

Potential Losses from Leading As a Facilitator

Leading a group as a facilitator also has the potential to yield losses, including the following:

- Some of the decisions and/or recommendations issued by the group may not be ones that the leader wanted.
- It can take longer for decisions and recommendations to be issued than if the leader leads as a dictator.
- You'll have to invest more time and energy in your relationships with group members than you will if you lead as a dictator.

Computing the Ratio

When you compute a subjective benefit/loss ratio for each of these two styles of leadership for a particular group (i.e., committee, organization) with which you're involved, you're likely to conclude that the facilitator style yields more benefits and fewer losses than does the dictator one. Much of the discussion in the rest of this chapter is based on the assumption that you'd come to this conclusion.

CHARACTERISTICS OF EFFECTIVE ADMINISTRATORS IN ACADEMIA

Some characteristics of effective leaders for groups in academia are dealt with in this section. The order in which they're considered isn't intended to suggest their importance. Most are also applicable to group members. My primary source for this discussion was Covey (1992).

Few persons who are effective as leaders in academia have all of these characteristics (many of which, incidentally, can be cultivated). However, the more of them you have, the more likely you are to be effective when serving in this role.

They're Both Open to and Enthusiastic about Learning New Things

They stay current in their own field and related ones and use the information they acquire creatively to facilitate problem solving in the groups with which they're involved. They consider having to learn continually not a chore, but a delight!

They're Willing to Seriously Consider Solutions That Are "Outside of the Box"

They are creative themselves and do what they can to facilitate others being so. They encourage solutions being offered and considered that are "outside of the box." They believe that the failure to be creative in this way is learned behavior that can be unlearned to some degree. In other words, they believe that:

> Creativity is shackled by self-imposed constraints. Therefore, the key to freeing it lies in developing an ability to identify such constraints and deliberately removing them. (Ackoff, 1978, p. 9)

To experience how self-imposed constraints can limit options for solving problems, try to connect the nine dots below by four straight lines, without retracing a line or lifting your pencil from the paper.

The solution is at the end of the chapter.

Figure 5.1
Nine-dot puzzle

They Have Few Blind Spots

They rarely play "The Emperor's New Clothes" game while functioning in this role. That is, they rarely fail "to see things as they are in actuality" (Goleman, 1985, p. 15). They're unlikely, for example, to applaud a recommendation from a committee that persons having their experience and training should be aware is impractical.

They're Willing to Be "Confused by Facts"

They rarely, if ever, communicate (directly or indirectly) the following message to those whom they lead: "My mind is made up and I don't want to be confused by facts." They accept the basic tenet of the scientific method that all conclusions (facts) are tentative and subject to change whenever new information becomes available.

They're Service-Oriented

They consider employment in academia to be a mission (calling), not a career. They are "persons for others." They delight in helping others achieve goals. Their mission statement for life (see Covey, Merrill & Merrill, 1994) includes having the world, in some small way(s), be a little better because of their having been here.

They Radiate Positive Energy

According to Covey (1992, p. 34), their countenances "are cheerful, pleasant, happy. Their attitude is optimistic, positive, upbeat. Their spirit is enthusiastic, hopeful, believing." They're more likely than otherwise to believe that they can accomplish their mission, which can become a self-fulfilling prophesy.

They Don't Overreact to Criticism

After reacting briefly to it emotionally, they tend to regard criticism of their ideas and/or actions as input that can be helpful for refining them. They don't react with excessive defensiveness to criticism. They thoughtfully evaluate it and if they believe after doing so that it isn't valid, they continue to believe and/or act as they did previously. They're willing, if it's necessary to promote their ideas and/or recommendations for action, to do what Thoreau referred to metaphorically as stepping to the music of a different drummer.

They Create a Climate for Growth and Opportunity

They believe in the potential of the persons whom they lead to grow, and they provide them opportunities to do so. They applaud their achievements, rather than reacting to them with more than momentary professional envy and jealousy.

They Have a Multivalued Rather Than a Two-Valued Orientation

They aren't overly perfectionistic. They tend to interpret and react to events as if they existed in shades of gray rather than in just black and white. Consequently, their recommendations tend to be more doable than they'd probably be otherwise (i.e., you're more likely to be successful if your goal is to reduce the magnitude of a problem than if it's to completely solve the problem).

They're Flexible and Pragmatic

They advocate their points of view strongly and, at the same time, they realize that they're unlikely to get everything they want at once. So they're flexible and exhibit a willingness to compromise, and encourage those who disagree with them to do the same. They're pragmatic in that they'll take what they can get now and plan to go for more later. They realize that achieving their ultimate goal is likely to take some time and require a number of small victories rather than one large one.

They're Change Catalysts

They improve almost any situation they get into. They do this, in part, by building on their strengths and striving to complement their weaknesses with the strengths of others. If they are the chairperson of a committee, for example, they're likely to delegate tasks they don't do well to members who both do them well and enjoy doing them. And they usually don't feel threatened by having to acknowledge that members of their committee can do certain tasks better than they can.

ATTRIBUTES OF COMMUNICATION THAT FACILITATE MEETING ADMINISTRATIVE (LEADERSHIP) RESPONSIBILITIES

A necessary condition for success in meeting any administrative or other leadership responsibility is being able to communicate effectively.

Communication that's effective tends to manifest certain attributes. Some are dealt with in this section. The order in which they're considered isn't intended to be indicative of their importance.

Participants Behave in Ways That Communicate They Respect and Trust Each Other

For communication to be effective in facilitating group problem solving, all participants in the process must respect each other as equals. The comments of full professors and instructors, for example, must be given equal consideration when making decisions. And the leader (e.g., the chairperson) must not attempt to coerce the others, either overtly or indirectly, into doing what he or she wants them to do. Few people do their best work when they feel they are being coerced!

Another prerequisite for effective communication is mutual trust. It must exist on several levels to maximize the likelihood that the problem(s) the group is trying to solve will be solved. These include the following:

- Trust that suggestions, particularly ones that are "out of the box," won't be rejected out of hand

- Trust that information being furnished is accurate (to the best of the knowledge of the person furnishing it)

- Trust that people will competently do the tasks they agreed to do

- Trust that information and deliberations that are intended to be confidential will be kept confidential (which, of course, is crucial for tenure and promotion deliberations)

Participants Listen to Each Other Attentively with Empathy

Participants in the words of Stephen Covey (1990) "Seek first to understand, then to be understood." Before reacting to someone's comment or suggestion, they seek to really understand it and where the person is coming from. And they expect others to really try to understand their comments and suggestions and where they're coming from before reacting to them. Such listening may enable them to identify one or more areas of disagreement on which they'll be able to reach a compromise through negotiation.

Participants Communicate Messages Directly and Unambiguously

Participants make their comments and recommendations directly in language that can be easily understood by all present. And they realize when doing so that a message that's clear to them may not be clear to all because one or more of those present may lack some of the background necessary to understand it fully. Furthermore, they avoid professional jargon whenever possible, particularly that whose meaning isn't even close to being unambiguous.

Participants Bring Assumptions into the Open

Participants are both aware of and understand the assumptions underlying the various positions on each issue and recommendation being dealt with. Their deliberation on an issue or recommendation focuses mainly on trying to eliminate differences between the assumptions underlying it. This is done by presenting evidence in a way that can enable participants to change their mind without losing face. In some cases, of course, they'll be unable to resolve differences between assumptions and will, therefore, have to agree to disagree.

Participants Recognize Their Stereotypes and Other Biases and Try to Keep from Signal Reacting to Them

Participants recognize at least some of their stereotypes and other biases and try to prevent their causing them to signal react to issues and recommendations. By *signal reacting,* in this context I mean reacting to issues and recommendations almost reflexively—that is, without giving them much thought. While it's unlikely that anyone can be successful in avoiding such biases all of the time, almost everyone is capable of learning to do so most of the time (see Johnson, 1946, for techniques).

Participants Seeking Win-Win Solutions

The best solutions to disagreements about issues and recommendations are win-win ones. These are solutions that result from compromises that cause almost all (perhaps all) participants to feel that they've won something. They're desirable because more participants are likely to buy into (not sabotage) them than they are win-lose solutions.

Dialogue Is Utilized Whenever Appropriate

Dialogue is a form of communication that has as its objective seeking mutual understanding (Yankelovich, 1999). The result of such understanding can be less conflict and more cooperation. Even if the points of view on an issue don't change, dialogue can lead to a deeper understanding of each and, consequently, greater respect for individuals advocating each. This, by itself, can lead to more cooperation. Most of what I've highlighted in this section as desirable attributes of communication are compatible with dialogue. See Yankelovich (1999) for further practical information on implementing dialogue.

TIME MANAGEMENT CONSIDERATIONS: PREVENTING ADMINISTRATIVE RESPONSIBILITIES FROM BECOMING OVERWHELMING

Administrative and other leadership responsibilities in academia can consume huge amounts of time. For some faculty, this is a benefit because they enjoy having this kind of role. For others, however, it isn't a benefit because it can prevent them from meeting other important responsibilities. For junior faculty, such responsibilities, to both themselves and their department, would include generating a teaching, publication, and grantsmanship record that's adequate for being tenured and promoted to associate professor. And for associate professors, such responsibilities would include generating a teaching, publication, and grantsmanship record that's adequate for promotion to full professor. Furthermore, for both associate and full professors such responsibilities could include maintaining a sufficiently adequate record for teaching, publication, and grantsmanship to survive a post-tenure review.

While your demonstrating excellence in administration and other types of leadership in academia is highly likely to be considered a plus by promotion and tenure committees, its highly unlikely to cancel out your weaknesses in teaching, scholarship, or grantsmanship. Consequently, it's crucial that you manage your time in such a way that you'll be able to develop or maintain adequate records for these while, at the same time, meeting your administrative and/or other leadership responsibilities.

I present some suggestions in this section for managing the time you spend on meeting administrative and other responsibilities in such a way that you're likely to develop or maintain an adequate record for teaching, scholarship, and grantsmanship. My primary source for this discussion, other than personal experience, is Covey et al. (1994).

Formulating a Personal Mission Statement for Teaching, Scholarship, and Grantsmanship

Many faculty have failed to develop or maintain an adequate record for teaching, publication, and/or grantsmanship because they've never formulated a "first approximation" of a personal mission statement for each of these responsibilities. Such mission statements are considered "first approximations" because they may have to be revised whenever a new opportunity or situation presents itself. Consequently, they identify tentative, rather than definite, destinations.

Your mission statements for each of these should reflect both your department and institution's expectations for you and your personal desires. If you don't meet departmental and institutional expectations for teaching, publication, and grantsmanship, you're unlikely to be tenured, promoted, or survive well a post-tenure review. However, there are likely to be many ways that you can meet these expectations, and your mission statements should specify how you intend to do so at present.

You should also formulate a mission statement for your administrative responsibilities. Such a statement is needed to establish priorities (see the next section, Balancing Urgency and Importance for Establishing Priorities).

Such mission statements are personal—not intended to be shared with others. Their content could make you seem selfish to your colleagues (because you aren't making it a priority to meet their needs) or trigger in them professional envy or jealousy. Also, it may be obvious from them that accomplishing your personal missions will require you, at some point, to seek employment elsewhere.

Once you've formulated a first approximation of a statement indicating your destination for each of these responsibilities, your next step is to identify at least the first few milestones (goals) for getting there. Their function is both to indicate what you have to do to make progress toward accomplishing these missions and to keep you on track for doing so. If your administrative and/or other leadership responsibilities are heavy, the time you'll have available to accomplish these missions will be limited. Consequently, you can't afford to waste time on activities that are highly unlikely to get you closer to the next milestone. And if you don't know what the milestone is, you're almost certain to waste some valuable time.

Finally, you're going to have to formulate a plan for getting to the next milestone on the path to your destination (i.e., fulfilling your mission) for teaching, scholarship, and grantsmanship. You may, of course, change it if you become aware of a new option for getting to a milestone or an unforeseen obstacle to doing so has to be overcome.

Balancing Urgency and Importance for Establishing Priorities

To find the time to develop or maintain adequate records for teaching, publication, and grantsmanship and to make progress toward accomplishing your goals in each of these four areas while meeting administrative responsibilities, you're going to have to establish priorities. Covey et al. (1994) have summed up what you'll have to do in three words in the title of their book on time management—that is, put "first things first." They recommend that you assign each task for which you're responsible to one of the following four categories to facilitate prioritizing it:

   I. Urgent and important

   II. Not urgent and important

   III. Urgent and not important

   IV. Not urgent and not important

They also make a number of recommendations for assigning tasks to these categories, some of which are summarized here. First, they recommend that your judgment of a task's importance be based on your mission statements. Tasks that facilitate your reaching milestones should be assigned a higher priority than those that don't do so. And, not surprisingly, they recommend that tasks that don't contribute to your reaching a milestone should be avoided whenever possible. It may not, of course, be possible to completely avoid them if they contribute significantly to one or more of your colleagues reaching a milestone (e.g., helping to assemble a dossier for tenure).

A second recommendation they make is not to consider a task urgent simply because somebody claims that it is. Most tasks you're asked to do are considered urgent by somebody. Many junior faculty fail to develop records for teaching, publication, and grantsmanship that are adequate to be tenured because they spend too much time doing tasks that others consider urgent. While being very accommodating to students and colleagues can win you friends, it can't compensate for an inadequate teaching, publication, and/or grantsmanship record when you go up for tenure and/or promotion.

A third recommendation they make is to avoid spending time on Category IV (i.e., not urgent and not important) activities. Some faculty spend much of their time on campus gossiping with colleagues and students and being immersed in departmental politics. While time spent in these ways is usually more enjoyable than that spent preparing articles and grant applications, investing it in publishing and grant writing is more likely to yield long-term benefits.

The authors also make a number of other recommendations for time management that can facilitate your fulfilling the teaching, publication, and grant writing requirements for tenure and/or promotion.

The Half-Hour-A-Day Solution for Meeting Publication and Grantsmanship Expectations

If you have a full faculty load, including administrative responsibilities, you're likely to have difficulty finding large blocks of time for writing articles, books, or grants (and possibly, also, for doing the preparation necessary to teach better than just adequately). There is a solution that has worked well for me and many others in academia. This is to devote a half hour or so a day, every day, to working on such writing projects. I've been doing this for about 30 years and it has enabled me to author more than 20 books and more than 100 journal articles. My writing time, incidentally, is usually early morning (because I'm a morning person). For how-to information about functioning in this way, see Silverman (1998a).

The main objection that colleagues have raised when I've suggested they try this method is that their personal and professional obligations make it impossible for them to find a half hour a day to devote to writing. Assuming that you want to meet publication and grant writing requirements for tenure and/or promotion, then the appropriate priority for doing so would probably be Category II (not urgent and important). You're likely to be able to find the time by getting up a half hour earlier (or going to sleep a half hour later if you're an "evening person") or cutting back on doing Category III (urgent and not important) or Category IV (not urgent and not important) activities, particularly the latter.

I recognize, of course, that some faculty load themselves up with administrative and teaching responsibilities to have an excuse for not publishing and/or seeking grants. They believe, consciously or unconsciously, that if they attempt to engage in one or both of these activities, they'll fail. While this excuse for having a less than adequate publication and/or grantsmanship record may be acceptable to their colleagues, it's unlikely to be to an institutional promotion and tenure committee, particularly one at a university that is or is striving to become a research institution.

The Art of Saying "No"

Many people (including me) have a difficult time saying "no" when asked to take on a responsibility that, for them (but not, of course, the person asking), would be in Category III (urgent and not important) or Category IV (not urgent and not important). The consequence of their not doing so could be having insufficient time to meet their own Category I (urgent and important) or Category II (not urgent and important) responsibilities. All such requests, of course, cannot be refused for "political reasons." Nevertheless, many probably both can and should be.

Perhaps the best way to refuse such a responsibility is to be assertive and communicate, both straightforwardly and respectfully, that your present commitments preclude your having the time to do it. You, of course, may have to resist attempts by the person to bully you into accepting it. And if the person is a colleague, he or she may view you as being less than collegial for doing so. However, this consequence is likely to yield you a more favorable benefit/loss ratio than would having a less than adequate publication or grantsmanship record when going up for tenure and/or promotion.

SOME DO'S AND DON'TS FOR BEING PERCEIVED AS COLLEGIAL WHILE LEADING

Whenever you assume a leadership role in your department or institution, you place yourself at risk for having your collegiality questioned. While this risk can't be eliminated, it can be minimized. The following are some suggestions for doing so:

- Have a clear sense of the group's mission, and be well organized.
- Follow the Golden Rule (i.e., "Do unto others what you would have them do unto you" or "Don't do to others what's hateful to you"), but take into consideration when doing so that what you consider hateful another person may not and vice versa (see Alessandra & O'Connor, 1994, for a discussion of some implications of this for interpreting the Golden Rule).
- Be respectful to *all* of those whom you lead.
- Treat *all* of those whom you lead fairly.
- Do your fair share of the work.
- Express appreciation for individual member's contributions to the group accomplishing its mission.
- Don't hold unnecessary meetings or assign group members busywork.

SOLUTION FOR THE NINE-DOT PUZZLE

Figure 5.2
Nine-dot puzzle solution

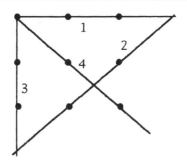

Chapter 6

GETTING PROGRAM GRANTS AND OTHER EXTRAMURAL FUNDING FOR YOUR DEPARTMENT AND INSTITUTION

Having a history of success in securing extramural funding (i.e., grants from government agencies, foundations, or corporations) and being likely to continue having success doing so are requirements for being tenured and/or promoted in many departments. In some of them, the amount of grant funding you'd have secure to meet this requirement is substantial—securing relatively small grants wouldn't do it. And in such departments, having no need for such funding in order to be productive and respected nationally as a scholar is unlikely to excuse you from meeting this requirement.

In departments and institutions that don't have success in grantsmanship as a requirement for tenure and/or promotion, being successful in securing extramural funding is likely to be regarded as a huge plus by members of the institution's promotion and tenure committee. In fact, they're likely to regard even the receipt of relatively small amounts of extramural funding in this way.

My primary focus in this chapter is on the potential benefits and losses to the recipient of the grant, students in the department, other faculty in the department, the department itself, and the institution from success in grantsmanship being a requirement for tenure and/or promotion. Some suggestions for maximizing the likelihood of being successful in securing such funding are given as well.

WHY THIS REQUIREMENT?

There is both a simple and a complex answer to this question. The simple answer is that if a faculty member needs more than a few hundred (or possibly a few thousand) dollars to fund one of his or her scholarly projects or special programs, he or she can't expect the college or university to provide the funding. Consequently, the faculty member will have to secure a grant from an outside (extramural) source to fund the project or program. The institution will, however, provide staff support for preparing the proposal and possibly seed money for a pilot (exploratory) project that's needed to make the proposal competitive.

This is certainly a valid reason for faculty to be expected to secure extramural funding. And many faculty do need such funding to meet departmental and institutional publication requirements for tenure and promotion and to create innovative teaching and other kinds of programs (e.g., community outreach ones).

But there is also a need for a more complex answer to this question, because faculty who don't need extramural funding to support their scholarly and other activities may have to secure it anyway if they want to be supported by their colleagues for tenure and/or promotion. In some departments and colleges, a history of success in grantsmanship is a formal requirement for tenure and promotion and in others this requirement is understood, but unstated (i.e., it is a gentleman's agreement).

For such a requirement to be so widely adopted, it must be yielding benefits other than the one of enabling faculty to pursue certain research projects and programs. And if it's yielding other benefits, it may also be yielding some losses. Some of the potential benefits and losses that can result from having success in grantsmanship as a requirement for being tenured and promoted are indicated here.

Potential Benefits and Losses for the Recipient of the Grant

This grantsmanship requirement has the potential to yield both benefits and losses for a faculty member who is the recipient of a grant. Some are indicated in this section.

The obvious benefit to the faculty member is being able to pursue a research project or undertake a program in which he or she is interested. And having the ability to do so can, of course, facilitate generating an adequate publication and service record (and possibly even a teaching one) for tenure and/or promotion.

There are also other benefits that a faculty member could derive from the receipt of such a grant, including the following:

- A reduced teaching load during the academic year (assuming that the grant pays a portion of his or her salary)
- A summer salary
- Funding for travel expenses
- Funding for equipment and supplies
- Funding for clerical assistance
- Funding for one or more research assistants
- Suggestions from reviewers of the proposal for improving the project or program
- Acquiring new information and skills
- Becoming better known nationally, thereby having more opportunities to contribute to scholarship at this level (e.g., being asked to referee papers and grant proposals and receiving invitations to participate in national and international conferences)
- Being more valued by your chairperson, dean, and vice president for academic affairs (and possibly others in your institution's upper administration)
- Receiving higher merit salary increases than you would otherwise
- Receiving better paying job offers from other universities (particularly if you'd be able to transfer your grant[s] to them)
- Pleasure!

A faculty member can lose, as well as benefit, from having to meet this grantsmanship requirement. Perhaps the main way that he or she can lose is by being unable to pursue his or her scholarly or other academically relevant interests because of the time required to both seek grants and, if they're secured, do the projects or conduct the programs that were described in the proposals for them. Doing these can be extremely time consuming.

Why might having to meet this requirement prevent a faculty member from pursuing his or her scholarly or other academically relevant interests? There could be at least two reasons. First, the project or program may be one for which extramural funding isn't necessary. For example, it may be a meta-analysis (see Silverman, 1998b) of existing data for which the faculty member already has the necessary hardware (computer) and software. Or it may be an academic book for which the advance will cover expenses. Or it may be the development of a program that the institution is willing to fund (at least initially).

A second reason why having to meet this requirement might prevent a faculty member from pursuing his or her scholarly or other academically relevant interests is that there may be no government granting agency, foundation, or corporate grant program that would likely provide funding at this time. There may be a grant program that is somewhat of a match, but securing funding from it would be a real long shot. Preparing a proposal for such a project or program can consume many hours, hours that could be spent on the project itself, assuming, of course, that it's doable without extramural funding.

There are also other potential losses that a faculty member could experience from having to meet this requirement, including the following:

- Having to spend huge amounts of time seeking funding for and doing projects or managing programs in which he or she has no real interest (their only real virtue being that they were fundable)
- Having to delay doing a project that can be done without extramural funding until securing extramural funding, or doing the project and then having to be dishonest when seeking a grant for it
- Feeling more like a cash cow than a scholar

Potential Benefits and Losses for the Students in the Department

Some of the students in a department may be able to benefit, directly or indirectly, from a member of its faculty securing a grant. If the grant is a training one, they may be able to get some of their tuition paid for. And if the grant is a research one, the possible benefits include the following:

- Graduate students may be able to get research assistantships that are funded by the grant.
- Both undergraduate and graduate students may have access to equipment that they wouldn't have access to otherwise (i.e., equipment purchased by the grant).
- Both undergraduate and graduate students may be able to assist with the research as a learning experience.
- Graduate students may be able to do parts of the research for the project as theses or dissertations.

About the only ways that students could lose by a professor in their department having a grant is if the professor's involvement with the grant takes time away from the students and/or if the professor takes time in class to talk about the grant when doing so isn't relevant.

Potential Benefits and Losses for Other Faculty

Some members of a department's faculty may get benefits or losses from one of their number securing a grant, particularly a fairly large one. The potential benefits may include one or more of the following:

- One or more of the other faculty may be able to collaborate with the person who received the grant on some of the research.
- Some of the funding given the institution for indirect (overhead) costs may be returned to the department to provide seed money for other faculty member's research projects.
- Equipment purchased for the project with grant funds may also be usable by other faculty for their research.
- Graduate students whose research assistantships are funded by the grant may do their theses or dissertations with other faculty because of being more interested in their specialties.

Unfortunately, a member of a department getting a grant (particularly a substantial one) can bring about losses for one or more of its other faculty. Such losses may include one or both of the following:

- A loss of prestige in the department because of having considerably smaller grants
- Having fewer opportunities to direct theses and dissertations

Potential Benefits and Losses for the Department Itself

A department, as a whole, can both benefit and lose by one of its members securing a grant, particularly a relatively large one. The ways that it can (but not necessarily will) benefit include the following:

- Increased visibility and prestige within its institution (i.e., university and/or college)
- Reduced pressure from its dean and upper administration to secure extramural funding
- An increase in its operating budget (possibly by receiving a share of the indirect overhead costs paid to the institution by the granting agency)
- Greater visibility nationally in its field, which can help in recruiting students (e.g., by giving it a higher ranking nationally in surveys, such as those currently published annually by *U.S. News and World Report*)

- Aid in recruiting faculty who have, or are striving to develop, a national reputation in its field
- Increased financial support for its students, particularly its graduate students
- More learning opportunities for its students (e.g., by participating in ongoing research or getting experience using specialized equipment that was purchased with grant funds)
- Increased opportunities for securing extramural funding (i.e., the fact that department projects have been judged worthy of such support makes it less risky for others to support them)

The ways that a department, as a whole, can (but not necessarily will) lose by one of its members securing a grant (particularly a relatively large one) include the following:

- Having to find someone to teach one or more of the recipient's classes and possibly meet others of his or her responsibilities to the department if the grant pays a part of the recipient's salary
- Less collegial relationships within the department because of other faculty having to pick up the slack and carry a larger load, and/or professional envy and jealousy

Potential Benefits and Losses for the Institution

The institution (i.e., college or university) itself can both benefit and lose by one of its faculty receiving a grant, particularly a substantial one. The ways that it could benefit include the following:

- If the grant is a research one, it would contribute to reinforcing the image of the college and university with its accrediting association as being a research institution.
- Positive reports in the media about what the grant funded can increase the institution's visibility and prestige and, in this way, contribute significantly to its student recruitment efforts.
- Positive reports in the media about what the grant funded can increase the institution's visibility and prestige nationally and internationally and, in this way, contribute significantly to motivating alumni and others to support the institution financially.

The ways in which the institution can lose by one of its faculty securing a grant (particularly a relatively large one) include the following:

- The grant may not pay for any indirect costs, so the institution may have to do so. Or it may have to provide matching funds.
- Negative reports in the media about what the grant funded can damage the institution's reputation.

SOME SUGGESTIONS FOR MAXIMIZING THE LIKELIHOOD OF SUCCESS IN SECURING EXTRAMURAL FUNDING

There is considerable how-to information available that's relevant for grantsmanship in academia. Sources include books, journal articles, Web sites (particularly those of government agencies, foundations, and other granting entities), and institutional offices for research support. This section is intended to supplement this information by highlighting some issues it's important to consider when dealing with grants.

The suggestions in this section are based on my 35-plus years of involvement with grants, including applying for them, being funded by them, evaluating applications for them, and listening to knowledgeable people talk about them. With regard to the latter, the person from whom I've learned the most was Dr. Robert Moulton, Dean of the College of Education at New Mexico State University. Applications that he has drafted have yielded more than 20 million dollars in extramural funding.

Acquire a Mentor or Collaborator Who Has Been Successful in Securing Extramural Funding

Grantsmanship is a game. And, like all competitive games, it has rules and strategies for maximizing the likelihood of winning. Some of its rules are written, but others are unwritten. The same is true for strategies for maximizing the likelihood of winning at it (i.e., getting funded).

A person who attempts to play a game without being mentored by someone who's knowledgeable about its unwritten rules and strategies is likely to lose. The same is true for somebody who applies for a grant without such input. Consequently, if you're new at it you'd be wise to acquire a knowledgeable mentor, who may also be a collaborator, before applying for a grant.

Realize That Grant Programs Are Almost Always Highly Competitive

There are far more applications for most grants than can be funded. It's quite likely that at least a few of the projects that aren't funded really are worthwhile and worthy of being so. They may, in fact, be more worthwhile than some that are funded. Unfortunately, the decision about which projects get funded and which don't tends to be fairly subjective when the choice to be made is between ones that are both worthwhile and doable. While there are probably some guidelines, their interpretation is unlikely to be clear-cut.

That grant programs are highly competitive has at least two important implications. The first is that it isn't safe to interpret failure to fund a project as meaning that the project isn't worthwhile. While this certainly could be the case, there could be other reasons for a project not being funded, including problems with the grant application and the granting entity having insufficient funding for all worthwhile projects.

The second implication is that the project not only has to be worthwhile and doable, but it also has to be "sold" well to the granting agency. This implication is dealt with next.

Recognize That Attracting Grant Funding Is Largely a Marketing Chore

The fact that college and university faculty, other than faculty in colleges of business administration, have to be knowledgeable about and engage in marketing may be surprising to you. It may not seem dignified somehow for persons in academia to sell things. Yet, when you apply for a grant you're doing just that. That is, you're attempting to sell a product—a project—to a government agency, foundation, or corporation. And, if you're to be successful (i.e., get the grant), you're going to have to market it to them in a way that's likely to beat out the competition (i.e., the projects with which its competing for funding).

Your failing to recognize this reality can reduce the likelihood that your proposals will be funded, particularly if they're competing with ones prepared by persons who do recognize it. Certainly, no amount of marketing expertise is likely to get a poor proposal funded. However, marketing expertise can influence the decision about which of several good proposals gets funded. Many of the suggestions in this section are for marketing proposals competently.

Strive for a Favorable Semantic Reaction to Your Proposals

Objects and events, like words, have meanings. And their meanings are likely to be based on tacit knowledge (Polanyi, 1967). That is, we're aware of their meanings, but don't know specifically why they have them for us. An example that's used frequently to explain tacit knowledge is recognizing a person's face but not knowing specifically how one did it.

The reaction of a person to an object or event based on the conscious or unconscious meaning it has for them has been referred to as a semantic reaction (Korzybski, 1958). A proposal for a grant and the persons submitting it can be viewed as "objects" to which both the staff of the granting entity and those who referee the proposal will have semantic reactions. A positive semantic reaction to a proposal and/or a person who submitted it can predispose them to look favorably on the project described in it, and a negative one can do the opposite. Some strategies for maximizing the likelihood that the semantic reaction to a project will be positive are presented elsewhere in this section.

Highlight Benefits in Your Proposal, Not Features

One of the most common mistakes that academics make when preparing grant proposals is assuming that the benefits of the project described in them are obvious. Consequently, they say little, or nothing, about them. Instead they carefully document what they propose doing and their qualifications (and possibly also those of others who will be involved with the project) for doing it. And they stress the features of what they hope the project will yield but don't carefully document how its possible outcomes could benefit people.

One reason that the potential benefits from a project may seem obvious to you is that you've spent a great deal of time thinking about the project. Those who will be evaluating your proposal are unlikely to spend more than a few hours doing so. Consequently, even if they're specialists in your field, they're unlikely to be aware of all its potential benefits. And, worse yet, it's likely that at least a few of those who evaluate your proposal won't be specialists in your field, thereby making them even less likely to be aware of such benefits.

There is another reason why it's important to carefully document the potential benefits of a project for which you're seeking funding. Granting entities have been criticized for funding projects that seem to lack the potential to yield meaningful societal benefits. Consequently, they're likely to give funding priority to those for which it seems to be relatively easy to document such benefits.

Try to Avoid Triggering the Biases of Potential Reviewers

The evaluation and prioritizing of grant proposals is far from being a completely objective process. One reason is the conscious and unconscious theoretical and methodological biases (i.e., differing beliefs) of reviewers. You'd be wise, therefore, to identify at least some of the possible biases of potential reviewers before preparing a proposal and use language, whenever possible, that's unlikely to trigger them.

Don't Assume That Reviewers Will Be Familiar with the Background for or the Discipline-Specific Terminology in Your Proposal

More than once I've been responsible for evaluating a grant proposal in an area in which I hadn't specialized and with which I lacked familiarity with some of the technical jargon and in which the author didn't even attempt to provide necessary background information. Judging by what I've been told by colleagues, this situation isn't unusual. Although I was motivated to evaluate such proposals as objectively and fairly as I could, I hesitated assigning them a high funding priority because if the projects for which they sought funding weren't considered worthwhile by persons knowledgeable in the field, my assigning them a high funding priority would reflect poorly on me.

Don't Cause Reviewers to Lose the Forest for the Trees

I've reviewed proposals in which there was so much detail that I wasn't quite sure after reading them that I really understood what was being proposed. It's crucial, therefore, that there be a straightforward statement of the project, in language that someone who isn't a specialist in the field can understand, preferably on the first page of the proposal. It's also desirable that there be such a statement indicating the need for the project and the potential benefits it could yield.

Realize That the Process of Rating Grant Proposals Is a Highly Subjective One

Referees are usually required to rate grant proposals on the number of "dimensions," and some composite of their ratings is used to prioritize (rank order) them for funding. Judgments on some of these dimensions tend to be highly subjective. One such dimension would be the potential importance of the project's contribution to knowledge. A referee who believed that the project would increase our understanding of a phenomenon in which he or she was interested would probably rate the proposal at least a little higher on this dimension than would one who had no interest in this phenomenon.

This source of subjectivity, unfortunately, is one over which you'll probably have no control unless you're allowed to select the referees who'll evaluate your proposal. If a proposal isn't funded, if possible you'll want to determine the likelihood of this being the reason. And if it seems probable that it is, you'd be wise to again submit the proposal to the same or another funding entity.

Try to Avoid Applying to Inappropriate Funding Programs

An appropriate funding program is one that has funded projects similar to yours in the past and appears willing to give serious consideration to funding others. There are online databases and other resources through which you should be able to identify at least a few governmental agencies, foundations, and/or corporations that have previously funded projects that are somewhat similar to yours. Your institutional office of research support can be of considerable help in identifying such programs.

An appropriate funding program may also be one that hasn't funded projects similar to yours in the past, but one that you've been informed has expressed an interest in doing so. You'd be wise before preparing and submitting a proposal to contact the organization and verify that "serious consideration" would be given to a project like yours. I made the mistake early in my career of not doing such checking for a project: the outcome was wasted time and embarrassment for both myself and the foundation to which I had submitted the proposal.

Attempt to Establish a Relationship with the Staff of a Funding Program before Submitting a Proposal to It

If at all possible, you'd be wise to contact potential funding programs and informally present your project to their staff before preparing and formally submitting a proposal. There are at least two ways that you could benefit by doing so. First, if they tell you that they aren't interested in giving serious consideration to a project like yours at this time, you won't waste time and other resources by preparing and submitting a proposal. Second, if they indicate that they are interested in giving serious consideration to a project like yours, they may give you some suggestions for preparing the proposal that will make it more likely to be funded. And by doing this, they'll be buying into the project, which, in itself, should make it at least a little more likely to be funded.

Follow the Instructions for Preparing the Proposal and Application *Exactly*!

Far more proposals are submitted for most grant programs than can be funded. A strategy that some use to reduce the number of proposals they have to consider to a more manageable one is to eliminate those for which the instructions for preparing and submitting weren't followed exactly.

If the Grant Is Awarded, Negotiate the Contract Carefully

If a grant program offers to fund your project, you or your institution will have to negotiate a contract with it. The negotiation is likely to involve the budget that you proposed. Before agreeing to reduce or eliminate funding for one or more of the items in it, be certain that doing so wouldn't put you at risk for not completing the project. If it would do so and you can't get them to agree to fund the item(s), you'd probably be better off refusing the grant and seeking funding elsewhere.

Incidentally, your threatening to refuse their offer could persuade them that the items they seek to reduce or eliminate are important and motivate them to find a face-saving way to change their mind about funding them. They may be so motivated because they've already invested significant time and other resources in the project and/or it wouldn't be good for their image (internally or externally) to have an offer of funding refused.

If the Grant Is Awarded, Treat the Granting Agency As a True Partner in the Endeavor and Go for a Long-Term Relationship

If your relationships with the staff of the granting agency (particularly if it's a foundation) are mutually respectful ones and they're pleased with the outcome of your project, they may be willing to fund some of your future projects. The reason is that they can be more certain of a project you do being completed successfully and amicably than they can of a project done by somebody with whom they haven't partnered previously.

There are several ways that you could benefit from such a long-term partnership. First, you wouldn't have to continually invest time in searching for sources of funding. Second, they're likely to require less formal proposals for such projects than would funding entities with which you've never partnered. And third, having an entity that's willing to fund your projects long-term would tend to reflect well on you.

If the Grant Isn't Awarded, Revise and Reapply!

Proposals submitted to highly competitive grant programs are rarely funded the first time that they're submitted. A huge mistake many academics make is assuming that if a proposal isn't funded the first time it's submitted, it's highly unlikely to be given serious consideration by that program in the future. This is only likely to be true if the project was regarded as not worth doing by almost all of those who evaluated it. If the reviewers' concerns appeared to be mostly methodological ones, it probably would be sensible to revise and resubmit the proposal. It's not unusual, incidentally, for a proposal to have to be revised and resubmitted four or five times before it's funded!

Browse RFPs (Requests for Proposals) in Your Specialty

The types of projects that we've dealt with thus far are ones that are thought up by the person (or persons) who prepares and submits the proposal. Granting entities sometimes have projects they want done and issue *requests for proposals* (RFPs) for them. That is, the entity itself comes up with a project and seeks to contract with a person, team, or organization to do it. Most governmental RFPs and some foundation ones are announced on the Internet. You may be able to arrange to have your institutional office of research support alert you to RFPs in your specialty. Time spent browsing them could be time well spent!

Chapter 7

WAYS YOU CAN HELP YOUR INSTITUTION MEET ITS RESPONSIBILITY TO SERVE ITS COMMUNITY

A college or university is a part of the community in which it exists. There are a number ways that its faculty and staff can contribute to it being a good neighbor, including the following:

- Giving talks on your specialty to community organizations
- Teaching continuing education courses
- Serving as a consultant in your specialty for local businesses
- Serving as a resource for municipal and state governments
- Publicizing your projects through local media
- Serving as a consultant in your specialty for local media
- Developing and/or participating in programs at your institution for the community
- Serving as a volunteer for community projects
- Encouraging students to volunteer for community projects

Some considerations and options for doing each are presented in this chapter, along with a rationale for individual faculty investing time and energy in these kinds of involvements. The benefits that can result from helping your institution serve its community are presented as well.

WHY ASSUME THIS RESPONSIBILITY?

Even if you aren't required to contribute to enhancing your institution's relationships in its community, you could benefit in a number of ways from volunteering to do so, including the following:

- It could make you better known, both within your college or university and your community.
- It could increase support for you from your institution's upper administration (which, of course, could be beneficial when you're being considered for promotion, tenure, or a merit salary increase).
- It could increase your options for networking or publishing (e.g., a book I wrote was based on what I'd learned from taking on such a responsibility).
- It could enable you to augment your income (e.g., if you did consulting).
- It could make your professional life more intellectually stimulating and/ or enjoyable.

GIVING TALKS ON YOUR SPECIALTY TO COMMUNITY ORGANIZATIONS

Many community organizations want to have a speaker at some of their meetings in order to boost attendance. If there are subjects about which you could speak for 20 minutes to a half hour that would probably be of interest to the general public, you may want to consider giving one or more of these talks every year.

Some universities (including mine) publish a booklet every year listing the names of faculty who are willing to give such talks and the topics about which they're willing to speak. These booklets are distributed to community organizations. Few of these organizations, incidentally, have funds allocated for paying an honorarium. Nevertheless, such talks tend to be great PR for the institution (since they're usually advertised in local media) and enjoyable for the presenter.

TEACHING CONTINUING EDUCATION COURSES

There are two kinds of continuing education courses that a faculty member of a college or university could offer that would be likely to enhance the image of that college or university in its community. The first would be courses through which practitioners in the person's field could earn Continuing Education Credits (CEUs) for license renewal, at reasonable cost, without having to travel very far. These courses could be conducted under the auspices of the college or university or another institution in the community (e.g., a school system or corporation). A faculty member who teaches such a course should certainly expect to receive an honorarium for doing so.

The second kind of continuing education course would be one intended for the general public. It could deal with a topic in the faculty member's specialty or something unrelated to it. If the latter, it probably would relate to a hobby. (For example, I've been collecting cameras and other photography artifacts for more than 50 years and could offer a continuing education course on getting started with this hobby.) A continuing education course for the general public could be offered under the auspices of your college or university, a local municipality, a local high school, or a senior citizen's organization. The presenter of such a course is likely to receive an honorarium, but it may not be very large.

Offering such a course can be an enjoyable experience for the presenter. It can also be an intellectually stimulating experience for the presenter and possibly result in him or her learning as much as or more than those being taught.

SERVING AS A CONSULTANT IN YOUR SPECIALTY FOR LOCAL BUSINESSES

Some college and university faculty are able to both enhance the status of their institution as a good neighbor and supplement their income by being helpful to local businesses in their specialty. You're especially likely to have opportunities to do such consulting if you're one of the only persons in your community who has a particular kind of expertise that local businesses occasionally need.

Many colleges and universities encourage their faculty to do such consulting if it doesn't interfere with their meeting other responsibilities. They may even have a specific policy stating that faculty are allowed to spend a certain percentage of their time doing paid consulting (at my university it's one day a week). A college or university can benefit in several ways from encouraging its faculty to do so, including:

- Enhancing its image as a community resource
- Keeping its faculty who enjoy doing consulting happier
- Keeping its faculty up-to-date with regard to what's happening in their field in the real world

- Opening the door for internship opportunities for its students and/or employment opportunities for its graduates
- Recruiting a few students (e.g., children of those with whom the faculty member consults)
- Opening the door for the business to partner with it financially (i.e., partially fund one or more of its projects)

SERVING AS A RESOURCE FOR MUNICIPAL AND STATE GOVERNMENTS

Most colleges and universities encourage their faculty to function as appointed or elected public servants at municipal or state levels, so long as doing so doesn't interfere with meeting their responsibilities to their institutions. Having members of their faculty serve their community in these ways tends to enhance the institution's image as a community resource (i.e., if the college or university hadn't employed them, they wouldn't be available to serve the municipality or state).

There are a number of ways that a member of a college or university faculty may be able to function as a part-time public servant. These range from being elected to a local school board to accepting an appointment to serve on a governor's advisory commission.

You may be able to benefit in one or more of the following ways from being a part-time public servant:

- Having an opportunity to partially fulfill your religious commitment to be "a person for others" by making a meaningful difference in the lives of at least a few persons
- Adding a source of enjoyment and/or intellectual stimulation to your life
- Becoming more knowledgeable about certain issues
- Becoming better known in your community
- Acquiring new opportunities for networking
- Possibly supplementing your income (some such appointments are volunteer ones)

PUBLICIZING YOUR PROJECTS THROUGH LOCAL MEDIA

Members of communities identify with and share vicariously in the accomplishments of their institutions (e.g., their football, baseball, and basketball teams). Most colleges and universities have an office whose responsibilities include publicizing locally the projects and accomplishments of its faculty. They do so in both the institution's publications (e.g., alumni magazines) and the local print and electronic media (in part, through press releases).

You're more likely to be successful getting local media to publicize your projects and accomplishments by *partnering* with your public relations office rather than by expecting them to assume all of the responsibility for making it happen. They are only likely to have the time to adequately do so for what the institution considers major projects or accomplishments. Consequently, if you don't treat your relationship with this office as a partnership, you're unlikely to have much success getting publicity for your projects and accomplishments.

One way you can be proactive in such a partnership is to draft press releases that your public relations department can circulate to local media. You're really in a better position than they are to draft these because you're more knowledgeable about your projects and accomplishments, assuming that you can do so without being overly modest. If you use the standard format for press releases and deliver them to your public relations department in electronic form (i.e., by e-mail or on a disk), they can easily edit and circulate them. For practical information about creating press releases that stand a good chance to attract media attention, see Blake & Bly (1997), Dobmeyer (1996), and/or Gurton (2001).

SERVING AS A CONSULTANT IN YOUR SPECIALTY FOR LOCAL MEDIA

When an important story breaks in the national media, newspapers, television stations, and radio stations in your community may seek to interview a local authority about the topic with which it deals. Most faculty tend to be reactive, rather than proactive, toward giving such interviews. That is, they give them when asked, but don't directly promote themselves to local media as a person who gives them. They may, however, do so indirectly by having their public relations office send local media press releases about their activities.

DEVELOPING AND/OR PARTICIPATING IN PROGRAMS AT YOUR INSTITUTION FOR THE COMMUNITY

Most colleges and university sponsor a number of programs for persons residing in their community who aren't their students. They do so to build goodwill for themselves in their community and/or to provide practical experience (practicum) for their students. The following are examples:

- Saturday morning drama and art classes for children, particularly elementary school–age ones
- Sports clinics and camps for children
- Special summer "enrichment" classes for middle school or high school students, particularly for minority and/or gifted ones
- Medical, dental, rehabilitation, mental health, and educational clinics (to both serve the community and provide practicum experience for students)
- Laboratory schools
- Legal assistance clinics (to both serve the community and provide practicum experience for law students)
- Regional science fairs

You may find it both worthwhile and enjoyable to participate in an ongoing program of this type or to develop one. Doing the latter, incidentally, may enable you to attract extramural funding, thereby enhancing your grantsmanship record.

SERVING AS A VOLUNTEER FOR COMMUNITY PROJECTS

College and university faculty have generated goodwill for their institution by serving as volunteers in community projects that aren't sponsored by their institution. Two examples would be answering telephones for public television station telethons and helping to build houses for Habitat for Humanity.

ENCOURAGING STUDENTS TO VOLUNTEER FOR COMMUNITY PROJECTS

Encouraging students to serve as volunteers in their community can be beneficial to both them and it. My university's mission includes encouraging our graduates to become "persons for others," regardless of the field in which they major. Perhaps the best way we've found to facilitate their doing so is to encourage them to do volunteer work while they're students. Our experience has been that most discover fairly quickly that one of the most personally satisfying things they can do is to help others.

Chapter 8

WAYS YOU CAN HELP YOUR DEPARTMENT MEET ITS SERVICE RESPONSIBILITIES TO PROFESSIONAL ASSOCIATIONS

Almost all faculty belong to at least one state, national, or international association that's directly or indirectly related to their teaching, research, and/or writing. Such associations differ in a number of ways, including the following:

- The size of their membership (which can range from fewer than 100 to more than 100,000)
- The geographical confines of their membership (i.e., municipal, state, national, or international)
- Their annual dues (which can range from less than 50 to 200 dollars or more)
- Requirements for membership (which can range from merely having an interest in a topic on which they focus to possessing a specific credential)
- The complexity of their power structure (which can range from a few elected officers to a large elected legislative council, elected officers, and paid staff)
- Whether they designate their mission as being professional, scientific, scholarly, or a combination of these
- Whether their focus is an academic discipline, a segment of an academic discipline, or something that crosses disciplinary boundaries
- Whether they have a national headquarters and a paid staff

- Whether they have an annual convention with paper presentations and publish journals
- The extent to which they use the Internet for communicating with members

Our focus in this chapter is on potential benefits and losses to faculty and institutions from faculty involvement in such associations, opportunities for working toward achieving a leadership role in them, and strategies for doing so.

POTENTIAL BENEFITS TO FACULTY FROM INVOLVEMENT IN PROFESSIONAL ASSOCIATIONS

While faculty can both benefit and lose from actively participating in professional associations, the potential benefits from doing so are likely to far outweigh the potential losses. The following are some of the potential benefits from being active in such an association:

- Enhancing your statewide, national, and/or international reputation
- Enhancing your opportunities for networking and collaborating
- Enhancing your opportunities for disseminating research findings at conferences and conventions and publishing articles
- Enhancing your possibilities for receiving awards
- Enhancing your opportunities for travel
- Gaining a meaningful activity that's intellectually stimulating and/or enjoyable
- Reducing the likelihood that you'll experience burnout
- Enhancing your reputation in your department, college, and university

Why being active in a professional association has the potential to yield each of these is indicated below.

Enhancing Your Statewide, National, and/or International Reputation

Few persons in academia become well known outside of their specialty (or specialties). However, actively participating in a professional association whose members share your field is likely to make you better known within your field. If the association is a state one, then many of those in the state who share your specialty will probably belong to it;

the same is true for national and international associations. And if your contributions to the association are respected by most of its membership, your professional reputation is likely to be enhanced.

Enhancing Your Opportunities for Networking and Collaborating

If you're active in an association to which others with your interests belong, you're likely to meet at least a few of them at its conventions or conferences. Networking and/or collaborating with them could facilitate one or more of your scholarly or other professional projects.

Enhancing Your Opportunities for Disseminating Research Findings at Conferences and Conventions and Publishing Articles

Most academic associations schedule platform presentations, poster sessions, or scientific exhibits at their annual conventions to enable members to disseminate research findings. Promotion and tenure committees expect faculty to do such presentations. And being active in one or more such associations provides opportunities for doing them.

Many scholarly associations publish journals. It may not be necessary to be a member to have a paper published in one. However, if more acceptable manuscripts are received than can be published, priority is likely to be given to those of members, particularly of members who've been helpful to the association.

Enhancing Your Possibilities for Receiving Awards

Your receiving an award for scholarship or teaching can enhance your reputation both in your field and at your institution. A main source of such awards is professional associations. The following are a few of the awards that a professional association may bestow on deserving members:

- Fellowship
- Honors of the Association
- Best article published in a journal
- Best scientific exhibit at a convention
- An annual award for service to the association (that's likely be named for one of its previous, well-loved leaders)

Enhancing Your Opportunities for Travel

Most state and national associations for academics have an annual convention and most international ones have a conference every two to five years. Participating in them provides opportunities for travel that may be at least partially funded by your institution. Your unreimbursed travel expenses, incidentally, may be deductible when computing your state and/or federal income tax.

Gaining a Meaningful Activity That's Intellectually Stimulating and/or Enjoyable

I've been active and held offices in several professional associations, and I've almost always found doing so to be a meaningful activity that's both intellectually stimulating and enjoyable. Of course, to benefit in these ways, your participation in the association has to be more than paying your dues and receiving its publications. Strategies for becoming more immersed in the mission and governance of such an association are dealt with elsewhere in this chapter.

Reducing the Likelihood That You'll Experience Burnout

To minimize the likelihood that you'll experience burnout as an academic, you'll have to find activities in addition to your routine teaching and departmental responsibilities that are likely to keep you stimulated intellectually. One such activity is becoming deeply involved in the governance and/or mission of a professional association. I, and several of my colleagues, partially attribute not burning out after spending more than 25 years in academia to having such involvement.

Enhancing Your Reputation in Your Department, College, and University

Your involvement in a professional association, particularly if it's partially a leadership one, can enhance your reputation with your chairperson, your dean, and some in your institution's upper administration (particularly the provost or vice president for academic affairs). Of course, you'd have to inform them (or arrange to have them informed) about it for this to happen.

POTENTIAL LOSSES TO FACULTY FROM INVOLVEMENT IN PROFESSIONAL ASSOCIATIONS

As I've indicated previously, faculty can lose as well as gain from being active in professional associations. The following are losses that you could (but not necessarily will) sustain from being so:

- Being unable to find the time to conscientiously meet some of your other commitments
- Having to fund some of the travel and other expenses you incur
- Having to cope with the professional envy, jealousy, and anger of colleagues
- Family problems

Why a faculty member being active in a professional association has the potential to yield each of these results is indicated below.

Being Unable to Find the Time to Conscientiously Meet Some of Your Other Commitments

Being active in a professional association—particularly being involved in its governance—can be very time consuming. It you try to conscientiously meet your responsibilities to the association, you may not have sufficient time to do so for some of your teaching, committee, research, writing, and/or grantsmanship commitments.

Having to Fund Some of the Travel and Other Expenses You Incur

Neither the association nor your department may have the funding to reimburse you for all, or even some, of the travel and other expenses that you incur while meeting association responsibilities. If you have to do some unreimbursed traveling to meet them, the expenses you'll incur can be substantial.

Having to Cope with the Professional Envy, Jealousy, and Anger of Colleagues

If you assume a leadership role in a professional association, particularly the state or national one for your field, you're likely to have to cope with the professional envy and jealousy of some of your colleagues. Furthermore, you may have to cope with their anger if your time commitment to the association prevents you from fulfilling, or fulfilling conscientiously, some of your commitments to them. They may even interpret your not fulfilling them, or not doing so conscientiously, as a lack of collegiality—that is, not truly being a team player. Such an interpretation can, of course, cause you problems when you go up for promotion and/or tenure or have a post-tenure review (see chapter 12).

Family Problems

If your involvement with an association requires you to do some traveling or for other reasons results in your spending less time with your spouse and children than you did previously, they're likely to resent it. If your marriage is a shaky one, it could even precipitate a divorce.

POTENTIAL BENEFITS TO DEPARTMENTS AND INSTITUTIONS FROM FACULTY INVOLVEMENT IN PROFESSIONAL ASSOCIATIONS

A faculty member's department and institution can (but not necessarily will) benefit from his or her involvement in a professional association. The following are a few of the ways that they may do so:

- Gaining visibility in a field
- Attracting more contributions
- Attracting more students

Why a faculty member becoming prominent in a professional association has the potential to yield each of these benefits to a department or institution is indicated below.

Gaining Visibility in a Field

If the association is a relatively large one and the faculty member is the president, the reputation of his or her department in the field could benefit, particularly if it isn't in a large research university that is widely respected nationally. For example, its ranking in the *U.S. News and World Report* annual survey of departments in the field could improve dramatically.

Attracting More Contributions

One reason why colleges and universities want to have at least one nationally prominent sports team is because it causes some of its alumni and those in its community to bond with the institution. Such bonding is likely to yield at least a little higher level of alumni and community giving. A department gaining national prominence (e.g., by one of its faculty becoming president of the national association in its field) is likely to attract a higher level of alumni and community giving than it would otherwise for this same reason. The more respected a department appears to be nationally, the higher the percentage of its alumni who will both identify with it and support it financially.

Attracting More Students

The more students who want to major in a particular field who've heard of a department that offers a major in it, the more applications that department is likely to receive. And one or more of a department's faculty becoming nationally prominent in a field can dramatically increase the department's visibility to those interested in majoring in that field, particularly graduate students.

POTENTIAL LOSSES TO DEPARTMENTS AND INSTITUTIONS FROM FACULTY INVOLVEMENT IN PROFESSIONAL ASSOCIATIONS

A department and institution can also lose by having a faculty member in a leadership role in a professional association. The following are three ways in which this can happen:

- Having to pay for his or her overhead and/or other expenses
- Having to reduce his or her faculty load
- Having to cope with him or her receiving job offers from other institutions

Why a faculty member becoming prominent in a professional association could have one or more of these outcomes is indicated below.

Having to Pay for His or Her Overhead and/or Other Expenses

Many academic associations, particularly smaller ones, don't reimburse a leader's employer for the expenses it incurs on their behalf. These

expenses can include office space, telephones, postage, printing and photocopying, utilities, secretarial services, and traveling. In most cases,
however, if the person is prudent, such expenses will be unlikely to place
a real financial burden on the department or institution.

Having to Reduce His or Her Faculty Load

If a faculty member becomes the president (or possibly some other
officer) of a large professional association, he or she may have to do a
great deal of traveling and/or spend a lot of time in other ways fulfilling
his or her responsibilities to the association. This could result in the
faculty member requesting a temporary reduction in faculty load. Hon-
oring such a request is, of course, likely to have financial and/or staffing
consequences for the department and possibly also the institution.

Having to Cope with Him or Her Receiving Job Offers from Other Institutions

A faculty member can gain a great deal of visibility from being an
officer of a professional association. One consequence of this could be
job offers from more prestigious institutions. This is particularly likely
if he or she also has strong publication and grantsmanship records. This,
of course, is likely to be more of a problem for departments that are
striving to attract and retain faculty from whom they'll attain national
prominence than for those that already have it.

STRATEGIES FOR WORKING TOWARD ACHIEVING A LEADERSHIP ROLE

A requirement for being entrusted with a high-level leadership role in
most professional associations is "paying one's dues." This involves doing necessary tasks that are unlikely to bring you much glory. A relatively small percentage of the membership of most professional
associations is willing to make more than a nominal contribution to their
functioning. Those who indicate by their behavior that they are willing
to do so are usually mentored by one or more of an association's officers
for assuming a leadership role.

The ways that you can signal having a real interest in being an active
member of an association include the following:

- Volunteering to serve on a committee from which you're unlikely to get
  much glory for the effort you expend

- Attending annual conventions regularly and contributing to the discussions at sessions
- Attending open-business meetings at its annual convention and, if possible, making meaningful contributions to the discussion
- Contributing to its publication(s)
- If appropriate, volunteering to serve as the chairperson of a session or a presenter at its annual conventions
- If appropriate, volunteering to help with its newsletter, journal, or Web site

There, of course, are other ways to communicate an interest in being active.

TENURE AND PROMOTION IMPLICATIONS OF HAVING HAD LEADERSHIP ROLES IN PROFESSIONAL ASSOCIATIONS

Your having had leadership roles in professional associations could be an asset, a liability, or both when you're making a bid for tenure and/or promotion. It could be more of an asset when your dossier is being considered by the institutional promotion and tenure committee than when it's being considered by your colleagues. There are at least two possible reasons. The first is that your colleagues will be less impressed than will be the members of the institutional promotion and tenure committee because they know more about the association and your involvement in it. And the second is that one or more of your colleagues will evince professional envy and/or jealousy. They may envy you for having had such an opportunity or they may feel jealous because you had it and they didn't. Either could cause them, consciously or unconsciously, to not support your bid for tenure and/or promotion. Perhaps the best way to minimize the risk of such an eventuality is to maintain a low profile with colleagues about such leadership roles.

Chapter 9

THINGS YOU CAN DO TO ENHANCE YOUR DEPARTMENT'S REPUTATION

Enhancing a department's reputation can be conceptualized as being a two-step process. The first is adding something worthwhile to what the department has to offer and the second is letting potential consumers of what was added know about it. The more potential students and practitioners in your field know about the good stuff that a department has to offer, the more solid will be its reputation!

You may be able to contribute to enhancing your department's reputation in one or both of these ways. That is, you may be able to add something worthwhile to what your department has to offer and/or you may be able to make some potential consumers of an innovative program that your department offers aware of it. The program may or may not be one that you helped to develop.

WHY INVEST IN ENHANCING YOUR DEPARTMENT'S REPUTATION?

Failure to contribute sufficiently to enhancing your department's reputation is unlikely to keep you from being promoted or tenured. On the other hand, if you do contribute a great deal to enhancing your department's reputation, the odds that you'll be promoted or tenured are likely to be better than they would be otherwise, particularly if your publication record and/or grantsmanship record is marginal.

There are a number of other ways by which you may be able to benefit from making such an investment, including the following:

- Enhancing your reputation in your field
- Making one of your pet projects a reality
- Being considered a team player by your colleagues
- Becoming more visible to upper administration
- Acquiring some extramural funding
- Attracting a few high-level graduate students to mentor
- Pleasing your colleagues by contributing to enhancing the status of your department in its college (although professional envy and jealousy could keep this from happening)

INFORMING IS MARKETING

Making potential consumers aware of your department's offerings is a marketing task. A department's offerings are products. And like all products, if they aren't marketed successfully, the entity providing them is unlikely to survive. Colleges and universities are becoming more bottom-line oriented and as a result, programs that either don't attract or no longer attract adequate numbers of students are at risk for being terminated or downsized (e.g., losing faculty lines).

Many professionals, including academics, consider it unseemly to become involved with marketing (advertising) what they offer to potential consumers (e.g., students and professionals in their field). They equate doing so with marketing commercial products and services, such as automobiles and plumbing services. There are at least two reasons why this attitude can be harmful to academics and/or those whom they serve. First, it could keep some people who could benefit from a department's offering from doing so. Obviously, if they aren't aware it exists, they can't benefit from it. Effective marketing can both make them aware of the fact that such an offering exists and how they're likely to benefit from it.

A second reason why considering involvement with such marketing unseemly can be harmful to academics is that it may put their job at risk. As I've already indicated, low student enrollment in a program can result in it being either terminated or downsized. And untenured faculty are at greatest risk for losing their jobs in such an eventuality. Consequently, a case can be made for it being more important for an assistant professor to contribute to such marketing efforts than for an associate professor or a full professor to do so.

Some of the ways that you may be able to contribute to marketing your department and its offerings are indicated elsewhere in this chapter.

AUGMENTING YOUR DEPARTMENT'S OFFERINGS

You can augment what your department offers its students and others by adding either tangibles or intangibles. *Tangibles* would be programs or services. And *intangibles* would be things that enhance its image, or reputation.

Tangibles

The following are examples of tangibles that you may be able to add (or help to add) to your department's offerings:

- New certificate or degree programs for undergraduate or graduate students
- New courses for undergraduate or graduate students
- New practicum opportunities for undergraduate or graduate students
- New financial aid opportunities for undergraduate and graduate students
- New facilities or equipment for undergraduate or graduate students
- New workshops or other types of continuing education opportunities (e.g., online courses) for practitioners in your field or related ones (e.g., for license renewal)
- New services for children or adults in your community who have a particular physical, psychological, or educational impairment
- New enrichment programs (e.g., art or drama ones) for young children in your community

Intangibles

Almost anything you do that enhances your professional reputation also has the potential to enhance the prestige of your department in the minds of potential students. And the more prestigious they consider a department, the more likely they are to apply to it if they're good students.

Some of the ways in which you can indirectly enhance your department's reputation are the following:

- Doing workshops and convention (conference) presentations
- Authoring books and articles in professional association journals or newsletters (print or online)
- Doing cutting-edge research
- Attracting extramural funding for your scholarly activities
- Becoming an officer of (or otherwise contributing both significantly and visibly to the mission of) a professional association
- Winning an award for your teaching or scholarly activities
- Doing consulting statewide, nationally, or internationally
- Being helpful, whenever possible, to students majoring in your field elsewhere who contact you

MARKETING YOUR DEPARTMENT'S OFFERINGS

A necessary (but not sufficient) condition of your department's offerings to enhance its reputation is for potential students and others to be aware of them. As I've indicated previously, the process through which such awareness is created is marketing. The following are examples of marketing techniques that you can use to help create such awareness:

- Mention your department's offerings in talks you give off campus.
- Do a poster or platform presentation about one or more of them at the state or national convention of your professional association.
- Author an article about one or more of them for a professional journal or newsletter.
- Add a page describing them to your department's Web site, and also try to arrange to have links to this page placed on other relevant Web sites.
- Mention them, when appropriate, in your e-mail and other correspondence.
- Create a brochure describing one or more of them for the information package that's sent to students who inquire about your program.
- Try to interest journalists from local and/or national media in writing articles about one or more of them (e.g., by sending out press releases about them).
- Try to interest the editor of your institution's alumni magazine in publishing an article about one or more of them.

These, of course, are not the only techniques for creating such awareness.

One important thing to keep in mind when doing such marketing is to stress benefits rather than features. A report of a feature that's been added to your program is unlikely to significantly enhance the reputation of your department unless the benefits it yields to students or others is communicated unambiguously. There is a huge amount of marketing research that indicates people are attracted to products by the benefits they expect to derive from their features, not by their features per se (De Bonis & Peterson, 1997).

TENURE AND PROMOTION IMPLICATIONS OF CONTRIBUTING TO ENHANCING YOUR DEPARTMENT'S REPUTATION

Doing a little more than your fair share when contributing to enhancing your department's reputation can pay sizable dividends for tenure and/or promotion, particularly if one or more of the following applies to you:

- Your publication record is marginal.
- Your record for attracting extramural funding is marginal.
- Your teaching record is barely adequate.
- Your successes in teaching, research, publication, and/or grantsmanship may have caused some of your colleagues to be envious or jealous of you.

With regard to the last of these, the fact that you've been willing to be a team player in this way could outweigh any such negative feelings your colleagues have toward you—if they aren't too deep.

Chapter 10

DO'S AND DON'TS FOR DEVELOPING COLLEGIAL RELATIONSHIPS WITH COLLEAGUES

If your records for scholarly activity and grantsmanship aren't outstanding when you go up for tenure and/or promotion, the collegiality of your relationships with colleagues can affect whether you'll be successful, particularly if some of your colleagues question your collegiality. It's highly unlikely, however, that you'd officially be denied tenure or promotion on this basis (because of the possibility of litigation and/or a complaint being filed with the American Association of University Professors [AAUP]). Rather, the reason given would probably be a less than adequate teaching, publication, and/or grantsmanship record.

Perhaps the best insurance against a negative appraisal of your collegiality interfering with your being tenured or promoted is having outstanding records for scholarly activity and grantsmanship. A faculty member with such records would have to have an extremely poor record for collegiality for it to adversely affect his or her chances for being tenured and/or promoted.

The next best insurance against a negative appraisal of your collegiality keeping you from being tenured or promoted is interacting with your colleagues in ways that are unlikely to cause them to question your collegiality (i.e., being a team player). A number of do's and don'ts are presented in this chapter that can minimize the risk to you that they'll do so. They're mostly from observations I've made and conversations I've had during the more than 35 years that I've been employed in academia.

DO'S

This list of do's for maximizing the likelihood of being considered collegial (i.e., a team player) isn't comprehensive, nor is the order in which items are discussed necessarily indicative of their importance. Nevertheless, following these suggestions will almost certainly decrease your risk of having your collegiality questioned when you go up for tenure and/or promotion.

Direct As Much (or More) of Your Time and Energy to Your Average Students As You Do to Your Better Students.

Instructors who essentially ignore their average students can create real problems for their chairperson and dean (and possibly other administrators at their institution). At least a few such students are likely to resent (and justifiably so) being ignored and complain to them about it. Consequently, few chairpersons or deans would enthusiastically support a faculty member for tenure who treated average students this way, because if that person were tenured, they would probably have to cope with such complaints indefinitely.

Do Your Fair Share of Departmental Committee Work

Your not doing a fair share of committee work is likely to be resented by your colleagues, in part, because it makes more work for them. Their expectation if you were tenured would be more of the same. Consequently, they'd be unlikely to enthusiastically support your bid for tenure. And having such resentment, they would be unlikely to support you enthusiastically for promotion to associate or full professor either.

Treat the Faculty in Your Department Respectfully, Particularly the Senior Faculty

Over the years I've known of several instances in which an assistant professor didn't respect as a scholar one of the tenured faculty and communicated this to the person, verbally and/or nonverbally. Even if there was some justification for not respecting that individual's scholarly activities (or lack of them), this wasn't a wise thing to do for at least two reasons. First, he or she would be unlikely to get that person's enthusiastic support for his or her bid for tenure. And second, he or she could lose the enthusiastic support of others in the department because of this imprudent behavior being considered an impediment to the faculty working well together.

Maintain a Low Profile with Department Faculty about Your Accomplishments and Honors

You're likely to find that the benefit/loss ratio from sharing information about your accomplishments and honors with at least a few of your colleagues is unfavorable because doing so precipitates professional envy and/or jealousy in them. These feelings can cause them to not support your bid for tenure and/or promotion enthusiastically. Consequently, you'd be wise to maintain a low profile about your accomplishments and honors with most (perhaps all) of your colleagues.

While you're likely to gain more than lose by maintaining a low profile within your department for your accomplishments and honors, the opposite could be true outside of your department. News about both could enhance your reputation with your dean and upper administration. Having strong upper administrative support could be helpful if your bid for tenure and/or promotion is threatened by professional envy and/or jealousy within your department.

Use "I'd Appreciate It If . . . " Rather Than "I Want You to . . . " Language When Making Requests of Colleagues

If you make requests of colleagues in a polite manner (e.g., "I'd appreciate it if . . . "), they're more likely to do what you want than if you use demanding language (e.g., "I want you to . . . "). While with the demanding language they may feel that you're trying to control them and resent you for it, they're unlikely to feel this way about requests that you make politely because it leaves them free to not do what you ask. (Incidentally, the "I'd appreciate it if . . . " language also works great with one's children!)

Volunteer to Serve on College and Institutional Committees, and Do Your Fair Share of the Work While on Them

Volunteering for and doing a fair share of the work while on such committees can enhance your reputation with administrators and others outside of your department. Among the benefits that you could derive from such upper administration support is help, if needed, for coping with by-products of the professional envy and jealousy of some of your colleagues (e.g., their not supporting you enthusiastically for tenure and/ or promotion).

Be Helpful to Colleagues When They Make Reasonable Requests

One of my greatest sources of pleasure during my career in academia has been the opportunity to mentor (or otherwise be helpful to) colleagues, particularly junior ones. Consequently, I strongly recommend that you give serious consideration to doing the same. A likely side effect of your doing so, incidentally, is enhancing your reputation within your department as being a team player.

Establish a Reputation for Being Dependable (e.g., Usually Meeting Deadlines)

A trait that's valued highly in academia (and elsewhere) is dependability. Persons who almost always meet deadlines and otherwise do what they agree to do tend to facilitate the functioning of all teams, including departmental faculty ones (e.g., committees).

Conduct Yourself in a Professional Manner on the Job

Your professionalism, both within and outside of your department, can affect your department's reputation. This doesn't necessarily mean that your image has to be a super conservative one. You can project a professorial image while being warm and/or informal.

Conduct Yourself in a Manner That Will Minimize Your Risk of Being Accused of Sexual Harassment

It's important to recognize that you're at some risk for being accused of sexual harassment by both colleagues and students, particularly those of the opposite sex. While you can't protect yourself completely against such charges, there are things you can do to minimize this risk. One is to avoid touching them or making remarks to them that could be interpreted as being sexual. Another is to keep your office door open while counseling students of the opposite sex unless it's absolutely essential that it be closed (e.g., to ensure confidentiality).

Conduct Yourself in a Manner That Will Minimize Your Risk of Being Accused of Cultural Insensitivity or Discrimination

To minimize the risk of being accused of cultural insensitivity or discrimination, you'll have to monitor carefully both what you say about and how you treat students and colleagues who are considered to be minorities by our society.

Be Yourself—Not a Stereotype of How You Believe a Professor Should Appear and Behave

You can be professorial without having the stereotypical appearance and personality of a professor in films and other media! Playing a role that isn't you is likely to both be uncomfortable and reduce your credibility with students and colleagues.

Apply for Extramural Funding That Isn't Entirely Self-Serving

Getting grants that support departmental programs and students (as well as your projects) can enhance your reputation within your department (and possibly also outside of it) as being a team player. Applying for such grants (and not getting them) can do so also.

Make Yourself Available to the Media When Doing So Is Likely to Enhance the Reputation of Your Department, College, University, and/or Profession

Your giving such interviews is particularly likely to be appreciated by your colleagues if your comments aren't completely self-serving and enhance the image of the department. The potential benefits to you from giving them include enhancing your image within your department as a team player and your visibility outside of it.

Mentor Junior Faculty, Particularly New Hires, If They Seek Such Help from You

Being willing to provide such mentoring can enhance your image among your colleagues as being a team player. And if you love to teach, doing so is likely to be enjoyable because the individuals with whom you'll work will probably be highly motivated.

Make It a Point to Congratulate Colleagues for Their Professional Accomplishments

Showing support for your colleagues in this way is both appropriate and likely to enhance your image as being a team player. It's also worth doing by letter or e-mail to persons in your field outside of your department. So few people do this, in part because of professional envy and jealousy, that your message is likely to be remembered warmly for a long time. One of my most treasured possessions is a fan letter for one of my books from a leader in my field whom I had never met.

Offer Emotional Support and Possibly Other Help (e.g., Teaching a Few Classes) to Colleagues Who've Experienced a Personal Tragedy (e.g., the Death of a Spouse or Parent)

This is an appropriate thing to do if you view your colleagues as a second family and is likely to be both appreciated and remembered (e.g., when you're being considered for tenure and/or promotion).

Be Willing to Negotiate and Compromise

Your willingness to negotiate and compromise is more likely to yield win-win decisions (or agreements) than win-lose ones (see chapter 5). And your striving for win-win ones is almost certain to enhance your image as being collegial.

Be a Good Listener

Listening to truly understand others points of view can enhance your ability to facilitate win-win decisions and agreements (see chapter 5) and by so doing, reinforce your image as a team player.

When in a Leadership Role (e.g., a Committee Chairperson), Be a Facilitator, Not a Tyrant

Leaders who are facilitators are more likely than those who are tyrants to be considered collegial by their colleagues.

Try to Avoid Causing Colleagues to Lose Face

There is perhaps no better way to lose the enthusiastic support of a colleague for your bid for tenure and/or promotion than to cause him or her to lose face.

Respond Promptly to E-Mail and Voice Mail Messages from Colleagues

Your frequent failure to respond to messages could be interpreted by your colleagues as signaling that they're not very important to you, which would be unlikely to enhance their enthusiasm for your being tenured and/or promoted.

Conduct Yourself in Ways That Will Cause You to Be Considered Approachable by Colleagues

Behaving in ways that make you seem unapproachable is counterproductive if you're trying to establish an image of yourself within your department as being collegial and a team player. One way to communicate being approachable is to encourage departmental colleagues and staff to address you by your first name, if they feel comfortable doing so (see Welch with Byrne, 2001, for a rationale).

Choose the Departmental and Institutional Issues Carefully on Which You'll Stand Up and Be Counted

Give considerable thought to the possible consequences that taking a stand on an issue could have on your reputation for collegiality before engaging in a battle you're almost certain to lose. There can, of course, be issues about which you feel so strongly that you're willing to take this risk in any case.

Demonstrate Thoughtfulness toward Colleagues—i.e., Be Considerate, Sensitive, and Caring to Others

Follow the Golden Rule (i.e., "Do unto others as you would have them do unto you"), taking into consideration cultural differences in what is considered being thoughtful, considerate, sensitive, and caring.

Demonstrate Tolerance toward Opposing Opinions of Colleagues

You're less likely to have your collegiality questioned if you agree to disagree with colleagues whose opinions differ from yours than if you persist in trying to change their opinions after it becomes obvious that this is unlikely to happen. Even if you're successful in convincing them that your opinion is more valid than theirs, they probably won't admit it because doing so can cause them to lose face.

Foster a Sense of Community

Anything you do that facilitates the faculty in your department working well together is likely to cause your reputation as someone who is collegial and a team player to be reinforced and possibly even enhanced a little.

DON'TS

This list of don'ts for maximizing the likelihood of being considered collegial (i.e., a team player) isn't comprehensive, nor is the order in which items are discussed necessarily indicative of their importance. Nevertheless, following these suggestions is almost certain to reduce your risk of having your collegiality questioned when you go up for tenure and/or promotion.

Don't Refuse to Attend or Prepare Adequately for Faculty or Committee Meetings

I'm somewhat embarrassed to admit that this is something that I did occasionally earlier in my career. I assumed that if a committee meeting was highly unlikely to yield anything meaningful, I'd be doing more for the program by either skipping the meeting or doing minimal preparation for it and instead spend the time on a task that would be more likely to yield the program something meaningful. I failed to recognize that an important function of such meetings, perhaps at times their most important function, is to promote collegiality and foster teamwork. My collegiality, incidentally, was questioned for behaving these ways.

Don't Refuse to Direct Student Research

Some faculty, directly or indirectly, attempt to discourage students from doing research with them, particularly if the research that a student is interested in doing is not of great interest to them. Directing student research in many departments is considered to be a component of a professor's teaching responsibilities, and discouraging it can raise questions about his or her collegiality. One reason is that a faculty member not doing a fair share of directing student research means that others in the department will have to do more than their fair share of it.

Don't Refuse to Do Student Advising If All of the Faculty in Your Department Are Expected to Do It

If you refused to do your fair share of student advising, others in your department would have to do more than their fair share of it. This would tend to cause those who had to pick up the slack (and possibly others) to be at least a little less enthusiastic in their support for your being tenured and/or promoted.

Don't Be a Chronic Complainer

Unless you're a superstar as a scholar or attract large amounts of extramural funding, you are unlikely to have the enthusiastic support of at least some of your colleagues for your being tenured and/or promoted if you are a chronic complainer. There can be at least two reasons. First, some of the persons about whom you complain are in your department and they hear about you doing so. And second, it isn't enjoyable being around somebody who complains almost constantly, particularly if it's usually about things that neither you nor they can change.

Don't Become Enmeshed in Departmental Politics, Except When It's Necessary to Do So Defensively

Spending time doing so when it isn't necessary can cause those with whom you don't align yourself to be less than enthusiastic in the letter they write for your dossier when you're considered for tenure and/or promotion. Furthermore, it's time that you could be spending productively (e.g., on your research, grantsmanship, or teaching).

Don't Demand More Than Your Fair Share of Departmental Resources

Departmental resources include such things as secretarial services, photocopying, travel funds, equipment (including computer hardware and software), honorariums for outside speakers, and financial support for scholarly activities. If you get more than your fair share of them, some others will get less than their fair share. This scenario is likely to dampen support within your department, at least a little, for your being tenured and/or promoted. If your funding needs exceed those available from your institution, you should either fund them yourself or seek extramural funding.

Don't Refuse to Do Your Fair Share of Student Recruitment Activities

These are activities that few faculty enjoy (in part, because they often occur on weekends) but can be essential for your department to remain healthy. If enrollment in your department's courses drops below a certain number, it may be at risk for losing faculty lines, or, worse yet, being terminated. But if the department has been working proactively to recruit students, both outcomes may be at least a little less likely.

Don't Spend Hours at Your Office Gossiping

Almost all faculty spend some time in each other's offices gossiping. They do so because it's enjoyable. Some, however, spend an hour or more almost every day while they aren't involved with students or committee responsibilities doing so. If they have adequate records for scholarship and grantsmanship when they seek tenure and/or promotion, then their doing so is unlikely to be a liability. However, if their records for one or both are inadequate and they claim that the reason is not having adequate time, they're likely to be in trouble. Some of the hundreds (perhaps, thousands) of hours that they spent gossiping while on campus over the years could have been spent being productive.

Don't Be Territorial with Colleagues

Being territorial with colleagues includes discouraging them from doing research or publishing in areas in which you're trying to establish or have established a national reputation. It could also include discouraging them from developing teaching interests and expertise in your areas. In addition, it could include discouraging them from using equipment that the department purchased with its funds to facilitate your scholarly or other activities. Your having the reputation of being territorial could dampen the enthusiasm of at least a few of your colleagues for tenuring and/or promoting you.

I was previously in a department in which some of the faculty were very territorial. I probably could never have developed comfortably in some of the ways that I did as a scholar if I had remained there because some of the areas in which I've done research and authored books and articles overlapped some of theirs.

Don't Demand That Your Faculty (e.g., Teaching) Load Be Reduced If You're Expected to Publish or Apply for Grants

Some nontenured faculty who at the end of their probationary period have less than adequate publication and/or grantsmanship records expect these to be excused because they've had to carry a full teaching load. This excuse is highly unlikely to be accepted by the members of institutional promotion and tenure committees because they know that if a person who's carrying such a load manages his or her time well, he or she can at least meet minimum standards for scholarship and grantsmanship. A skill that you'll have to acquire if you hope to be successful in academia is being able to keep a number of balls in the air simultaneously.

There are a number of good books on time management. One that I've found particularly helpful is Covey et al. (1994).

Don't Refuse to Come to Campus on Days You Don't Teach to Attend Committee Meetings If at All Possible

Your frequently refusing to come to campus for this reason can cause your collegiality to be questioned or reinforce the reputation you already have of not being a team player.

Don't Be Insensitive to the Feelings of Colleagues When Commenting on Their Scholarship

You can critically evaluate a colleague's research, publications, and/or theories without being nasty! Few departments would have any enthusiasm for tenuring or promoting someone who had a reputation for being undiplomatic about a colleague's work unless he or she was a superstar as a scholar.

Incidentally, a person who frequently is nasty to colleagues in this way is almost always someone who has a poor self-concept as a scholar. He or she gets a short-term boost to his or her self-esteem by being hypercritical of (i.e., putting down) other scholars.

Don't Proselytize Colleagues for Your Religion or Other Deeply Held Moral/Ethical Beliefs

If you did this, you'd have to be a supreme superstar as a scholar in order for colleagues who had different religious beliefs to have any enthusiasm for your being tenured or promoted. Doing so probably would be considered inappropriate even at a church-sponsored college or university. I've been on the faculty of a Jesuit university for more than 30 years and have never observed nor experienced such proselytizing.

Don't Develop the Reputation of Being Somebody Who Once His or Her Mind Is Made Up "Doesn't Want to Be Confused by Facts"

To truly be a scholar, you'll have to accept the tenet of the scientific method that states that all conclusions should be considered tentative and subject to change whenever new information becomes available. Your colleagues will probably respect you more, rather than less, if you're willing to acknowledge having been wrong.

Don't Make Negative Comments to Students about Colleagues

If you make negative comments to students about your colleagues, they're likely to get back to them. And one way that they may try to get even is to not support you for tenure and/or promotion. You could also lose the support of some of your other colleagues because they fear you'll do the same to them.

Chapter 11

DOCUMENTING COLLEGIALITY AND SERVICE FOR PROMOTION AND TENURE

Most (if not all) colleges and universities expect there to be some documentation in dossiers for tenure and promotion for what they term *service*. Collegiality may be mentioned as a requirement for meeting service obligations or it may be an unwritten, but understood, requirement—that is, a gentleman's agreement. One reason why collegiality may not be mentioned as a requirement for tenure and promotion is that doing so can place the institution at risk for being accused of limiting academic freedom.

The institution's guidelines for documenting service and collegiality in such a dossier are likely to be more vague than those for teaching and scholarship (which are themselves likely to be quite vague). There could be several reasons. One is that almost all of the responsibilities that are considered a part of service and collegiality are usually given considerably less weight in promotion and tenure decisions than are teaching and scholarship. The main exception is grantsmanship. Another possible reason is that this requirement is usually only a significant factor in such decisions if the candidate has done them poorly. Doing student advising or committee work exceptionally well at most colleges and universities is highly unlikely to compensate, more than a little, for a marginal publication or grantsmanship record.

That said, it's important that you have the fair share of service responsibilities that you undertook (those that are likely to be considered when assessing your collegiality and service record for tenure or promotion) documented in your dossier. What this part of your dossier has to accomplish—and some of the ways that you and/or the person preparing your dossier can facilitate it doing so—are indicated in this chapter.

THE OBJECTIVES

Your primary objective should be to minimize the likelihood that readers of your dossier will have a negative semantic reaction to your record for collegiality and/or service. A semantic reaction is a response to an object or event based on its meaning to the observer (see Korzybski, 1958, for an in-depth discussion of semantic reactions). A semantic reaction can be either positive or negative. Spin doctors in politics, for example, use the media to interpret events in ways that tend to make them less likely than otherwise to elicit negative semantic reactions. Referring to loss of life during a military attack as "collateral damage," for example, is less likely to elicit a negative semantic reaction than is stating directly that innocent women and children were killed.

A secondary objective could be to maximize the likelihood that readers of your dossier will have a positive semantic reaction to your record for collegiality and service. There are at least two scenarios under which accomplishing this could be particularly worthwhile. The first would be if you were being considered for promotion to full professor. Evaluators of such a dossier are likely to be looking for a better than "doing a fair share" record for some service-related responsibilities, including leadership in professional associations and grantsmanship. The second such scenario would be hoping that a relatively strong record for collegiality and service would balance out some weaknesses in teaching and/or scholarship. This is probably most likely to happen if you have a marginal record for publication and can argue cogently that the reason is, in large part, your having had to take on a major administrative responsibility (e.g., being a department chairperson).

STRATEGIES FOR ACCOMPLISHING THESE OBJECTIVES

A number of strategies for minimizing the likelihood of a negative semantic reaction or maximizing the likelihood of a positive semantic reaction to the collegiality and service section(s) of your dossier are indicated in this section. They, of course, are not the only such strategies, nor is the order in which they're presented intended to imply anything about their importance.

Provide a List of Service-Related Responsibilities and Awards

You should list all the service-related responsibilities you've had, particularly ones that you've had since accepting a position at your institution. The listing for each should include the date it began and ended and any recognition (award) you received for doing it. It would also be a good idea to include a brief description of your contribution(s) to each.

The responsibilities that may be appropriate for you to include in your listing include the following:

Institutional

- Service as an administrator (e.g., department chairperson, director of graduate studies, or coordinator of clinical services)
- Service as a member or chairperson of a departmental committee
- Service as a member or chairperson of a college committee
- Service as a member or chairperson of a university committee
- Service as an academic advisor
- Service as an advisor for a student organization
- Involvement with student recruitment activities
- Involvement with faculty mentoring

Professional Association

- Service as an officer of a professional or scholarly association
- Service as a member or chairperson of a committee of a professional or scholarly association
- Fellowship or another award from a professional or scholarly association

Community

- Service as a member or chairperson of a governmental community (municipal or state) committee
- Service as a member or chairperson of a nongovernmental community committee
- Talks to community organizations (particularly ones for which you didn't receive an honorarium)
- Media interviews

- Consulting with businesses in your community
- Volunteer consulting with professionals in your field
- Volunteer participation in community projects (e.g., Habitat for Humanity or a public television station telethon)

Miscellaneous

- An honorary degree or other awards from another institution (e.g., an alumni recognition award)
- Listings in "Who's Who" type volumes

There may, of course, be other service-related responsibilities that it would be appropriate for you to list.

Provide Letters from Faculty in Your Department

Letters from a department's faculty are the primary source that members of promotion and tenure committees usually use to determine whether there's any reason to believe that a candidate's collegiality is less than adequate. They make this determination based on both comments in the letters that are in the dossier and the letters that are conspicuous by their absence. The reason they pay attention to the latter is that a candidate's colleague may refuse to write a letter for the colleague's dossier if he or she can't be supportive. The combination of less than enthusiastic support in the letters that are in the dossier and the absence of letters from key faculty is quite likely to raise questions that could doom a candidates bid for tenure and/or promotion, particularly if his or her records for teaching, scholarship, and grantsmanship aren't outstanding.

Provide Letters from Others

Letters from persons outside of your department can also be helpful for making the case that your service and collegiality are at least adequate. Persons from whom you might want to request such letters include the following:

- A few former academic advisees who seemed pleased with what you did for them
- A few faculty and/or administrators at your institution from outside of your department with whom you've served on committees or collaborated in other ways

- Persons who have a leadership role in professional associations with which you've been affiliated who can comment on your service-related contributions to them (e.g., as an officer or a committee member)
- Leaders of community organizations to which you've contributed your time and/or expertise (e.g., as a committee member or consultant)

There could, of course, be other categories of people from whom it would probably be helpful to request letters.

Chapter 12

SERVICE OPPORTUNITIES
BEYOND TENURE

Once you've been tenured and promoted to associate professor, both your opportunities for service and the reinforcement you'll receive from colleagues and others from pursuing such opportunities are likely to increase. Furthermore, your accepting such opportunities is likely to be given considerable weight if you decide to seek promotion to full professor. Opportunities for service can exist in your department, your institution, your professional associations, and your community. Some are indicated here.

POST-TENURE OPPORTUNITIES IN YOUR DEPARTMENT

The following are four service-related opportunities at the departmental level that either aren't available to an assistant professor or are considerably less likely to be so than they are to an associate or full professor. The order in which they're dealt with isn't necessarily related to their availability or enjoyability.

Becoming a Department Chairperson

While few persons enter academia with the ultimate goal of becoming the chairperson of a department, many end up volunteering or being volunteered to be one. Among the ways that people acquire this responsibility are the following:

- They seek this responsibility because they want to pursue a career in higher education administration.
- They seek this responsibility primarily because they want a new challenge.
- They seek this responsibility primarily because they want its prestige and/or power.
- They are volunteered for this responsibility by somebody (e.g., the previous department chairperson or their dean), possibly because their potential for contributing to the department and institution's reputation as a scholar seems limited.
- They are the only one in their department who is considered acceptable by both its faculty and the institution's administration to have this responsibility.

A department chairperson may view the position as a chore, a challenge, or some combination of the two. It's likely to be a chore if he or she focuses, almost exclusively, on the routine, day-to-day tasks that have to be done for the department to function efficiently. It's likely to be a challenge if he or she focuses, almost exclusively, on making its curriculum and/or its contributions to scholarship more innovative and widely known. And viewing it as a combination of the two would require him or her to focus both on routine, but necessary, tasks and on innovation. The department chairpersons I've known who seemed to enjoy their position the most were ones who viewed it as requiring them to focus both on innovation and on doing routine, but necessary, tasks.

Being a department chairperson, like all activities, can have a downside. The following are several losses that you could (but won't necessarily) experience if you accepted this responsibility:

- Having to cut back on your research and writing
- Having to work summers (i.e., accept a 12-month contract)
- Having to be on call 24/7
- Having to inform students who aren't making satisfactory progress toward a degree that they're being dropped from the program
- Having to inform junior faculty who aren't making satisfactory progress toward tenure and promotion that their employment is being terminated

- Having to waste time trying to do the impossible for students and colleagues (e.g., having to spend hours assembling a dossier for a colleague for tenure or promotion who has no chance of being successful)

Our focus, thus far, has been on becoming chairperson of your department. Another option you may have is becoming chairperson of a similar department at another college or university. You're particularly likely to have this option if you've developed a strong national reputation in your field as a scholar and you've had some success attracting extramural funding. This is, incidentally, one of the few scenarios under which you're likely to be seriously considered for a position at another college or university after you've become a full professor.

Becoming a Member of the Department's Executive Committee

Some departments have a standing executive committee on which only tenured faculty can serve. Departments that don't have such a standing committee are likely to create an ad hoc one whenever the need arises. My department, for example, doesn't have a standing executive committee; however, an ad hoc one was created recently to respond to proposed college changes in the requirements for promotion.

The role of a standing executive committee, incidentally, is to advise the chairperson on issues that either affect the department or have the potential to do so. Such issues could relate to any, or all, of the following:

- Merit salary increase
- Promotion or tenure
- Dropping students from the program
- Terminating junior faculty or other staff

Becoming a Chairperson of a Departmental Committee

The chairpersons of committees in some departments are almost always persons having the rank of associate or full professor.

Becoming a Mentor for Junior Faculty

Tenured faculty usually are not assigned this responsibility. They volunteer to serve their department in this way and are likely to continue doing so throughout their academic career. Among the benefits that they're likely to derive from doing it are the following:

- Pleasure from knowing that they've helped someone (i.e., from having been a Good Samaritan)
- An opportunity to pass on some of the "wisdom" they've acquired for surviving in academia to the next generation
- An opportunity to get to know the colleagues they're mentoring better and possibly developing friendships with them and/or acquiring allies who could enhance their ability to survive departmental politics
- Reinforcing their reputation as being collegial (i.e., a team player)

POST-TENURE OPPORTUNITIES IN YOUR INSTITUTION

The following are three service-related opportunities at the institutional (i.e., college or university) level that either aren't available to an assistant professor or are considerably less likely to be so than they are to an associate or full professor. The order in which they're dealt with isn't necessarily related to their availability or enjoyability.

Becoming a Dean or Another Institutional Administrator

Most persons who are deans or have another position in college or university administration that's usually filled by a Ph.D. did not begin their academic career having this as a goal. They evinced exceptional leadership abilities in their department, professional associations, and/or community that was recognized by one or more persons in their institution's upper administration, and they were encouraged by them to pursue this career path. While being tenured may not be a requirement for some such positions, almost all of those who have them are tenured.

It is possible to get such a position at another college or university. Most are advertised nationally (e.g., in the *Chronicle of Higher Education*) when they become available.

Becoming a Member of an Institutional Promotion and Tenure Committee

Being tenured is almost always a requirement for membership on this committee.

Becoming the Chairperson of an Institutional Committee

Few college or university committees have a chairperson who isn't tenured.

POST-TENURE OPPORTUNITIES IN ACADEMIC ASSOCIATIONS

The following are two service-related opportunities in academic associations that are more likely to be available to associate and full professors than to assistant ones.

Becoming an Officer in an Academic Association or a Member of Its Council

If an academic association is a national or international one, almost all of its officers and council members are likely to be associate or full professors. This is a little less likely to be true if an academic association is a state one.

Becoming the Chairperson of a Committee in an Academic Association

Associate and full professors tend to be favored over junior faculty for chairmanships of committees in most academic associations.

POST-TENURE OPPORTUNITIES IN YOUR COMMUNITY

The following are two service-related opportunities in communities that are more likely to be available to associate and full professors than to assistant ones.

Becoming a Consultant to Media and/or Industry in Your Community

The longer you've been at a particular college or university, the more aware of you the media and others in your community who occasionally have a need to interview or consult with an expert in your specialty are likely to be. Furthermore, the stronger your reputation as an expert in your specialty, the more aware of you they're likely to be. Consequently, associate and full professors tend to be consulted more often than assistant professors by both media and industry.

Assuming a Position of Leadership in a Community Organization

Professors tend to be respected in most communities. Consequently, your being one can facilitate your being elected to a position of leadership in a community organization, even one that's not related in any way to your specialty. Having such a leadership position listed in your dossier is likely to be more helpful if you're seeking promotion to full professor than it is if you're seeking promotion to associate professor, particularly if your scholarship and grantsmanship records are marginal.

ADDENDUM: POST-TENURE EXPECTATIONS FOR COLLEGIALITY

The primary focus in this chapter has been on post-tenure service opportunities. Since this is the first chapter that didn't deal exclusively with collegiality, you may wonder whether being perceived as collegial after you're tenured ceases to be important. It does not. The same expectations for collegiality apply post-tenure as applied pre-tenure. Possible consequences of not being perceived as collegial post-tenure are losing departmental support for promotion to full professor, receiving very small merit salary increases, and otherwise being treated in ways that are intended to encourage you to either seek a position elsewhere or retire.

REFERENCES

Ackoff, R. L. (1978). *The Art of Problem Solving.* New York: John Wiley & Sons.

Alessandra, T., & O'Connor, M. J. (1994). *People Smarts: Bending the Golden Rule to Give Others What They Want.* San Diego, CA: Pfeiffer & Company.

Becker, B. A. (2000). Legal Issues in Academic Advising. In V. Gordon, W. Habley, & Associates, *Academic Advising: A Comprehensive Handbook,* 58–70. San Francisco, CA: Jossey-Bass.

Blake, G., & Bly, R. W. (1997). *Elements of Copyediting: The Essential Guide to Creating Copy That Gets the Results You Want.* New York: Macmillan.

Covey, S. R. (1990). *The Seven Habits of Highly Effective People.* New York: Simon & Schuster.

Covey, S. R. (1992). *Principle-Centered Leadership.* New York: Simon & Schuster.

Covey S. R., Merrill, A. R., & Merrill, R. R. (1994). *First Things First.* New York: Simon & Schuster.

De Bonis, J. N., & Peterson, R. S. (1997). *Managing Business to Business Marketing Communications.* Chicago, IL: NTC Business Books.

Dobmeyer, D. (1996). *Competing Successfully for Media Coverage: A Guide to Getting Media Coverage for Non-Profit and Community Organizations.* Chicago, IL: Dobmeyer Communications.

Frank, K. S. (2000). Ethical Considerations and Obligations. In V. Gordon, W. Habley, & Associates, *Academic Advising: A Comprehensive Handbook,* 44–57. San Francisco, CA: Jossey-Bass.

Goleman, D. (1985). *Vital Lies, Simple Truths: The Psychology of Self-Deception.* New York: Simon & Schuster.

Gordon, V. (1992). *Handbook of Academic Advising.* Westport, CT: Greenwood Press.

Gordon, V., Habley, W., & Associates (2000). *Academic Advising: A Comprehensive Handbook.* San Francisco, CA: Jossey-Bass.

Gurton, A. (2001). *Press Here!: How to Develop Good Relationships with Journalists and Achieve Positive Editorial Publicity.* London, England: Prentice Hall/Pearson Education.

Habley, W. (2000). Current Practices in Academic Advising. In V. Gordon, W. Habley, & Associates, *Academic Advising: A Comprehensive Handbook,* 35–43. San Francisco, CA: Jossey-Bass.

Johnson, W. (1946). *People in Quandaries.* New York: Harper & Brothers.

Josephson, M. (1988). "Teaching Ethical Decision Making and Principled Reasoning." *Ethics: Easier Said Than Done, 1(1),* 27–33.

Korzybski, A. (1958). *Science and Sanity: An Introduction to Non-Aristotelian Systems and General Semantics.* Lakeville, CT: Institute of General Semantics.

Kosko, B. (1993). *Fuzzy Thinking: The New Science of Fuzzy Logic.* New York: Hyperion.

Lundy, J. L. (1994). *Teams: How to Develop Peak Performance Teams for World-Class Results.* Chicago, IL: The Dartnell Corporation.

Polanyi, M. (1967). *The Tacit Dimension.* Garden City, NY: Doubleday Anchor Books.

Prosser, W. L. (1971). *Law of Torts,* 4th ed. St. Paul, MN: West Publishing Company.

Silverman, F. H. (1998a). *Authoring Books and Materials for Students, Academics, and Professionals.* Westport, CT: Praeger.

Silverman, F. H. (1998b). *Research Design and Evaluation in Speech-Language Pathology and Audiology,* 4th ed. Boston, MA: Allyn & Bacon.

Silverman, F. H. (1999). *Publishing for Tenure and Beyond.* Westport, CT: Praeger.

Silverman, F. H. (2001). *Teaching for Tenure and Beyond: Strategies for Maximizing Your Student Ratings.* Westport, CT: Bergin & Garvey.

Silverman, F. H., & Moulton, R. (2002). *The Impact of a Unique Cooperative American University USAID Funded Speech Pathologist, Audiologist, and Deaf Educator B.S. Degree Program in the Gaza Strip.* Lampeter, Ceredigion, Wales, UK: The Edward Mellen Press, Ltd.

Welch, J., with Byrne, J. A. (2001). *Jack: Straight from the Gut.* New York: Warner Business Books.

Yankelovich, D. (1999). *The Magic of Dialogue: Transforming Conflict into Cooperation.* New York: Simon & Schuster.

Zelditch, M. (1990, March). *Mentor Roles.* Proceedings of the 32nd Annual Meeting of the Western Association of Graduate Schools, Tempe, AZ, p. 11.

INDEX

About the Author

FRANKLIN SILVERMAN is a Professor of Speech Pathology, Marquette University.